The Widower's Guide
to a New Life

Joanna Romer

For information, contact
MSI Press
1760-F Airline Highway, #203
Hollister, CA 95023

Cover designed by CDL Services

Library of Congress Control Number 2013951735

ISBN: 978-1-933455-48-8

Once again, for Jack

Acknowledgements

I would like to thank the widowers listed below who gave me their time and their inspiring stories: Harry Abbott, Doug Bell, Rick Bernhard, "Bo" Bowman, Jack Don, Lewis Green, Dennis Hansen, Clancy Head, Walter Johnson, George Lane, Guerrino Lucas and Bob Murray. Without them, this book would not have been written.

Also I would like to thank the following people for their help and loving support with my writing: Victoria Barr, Carole Duncan, Cheryl Vassiliadis, Paula McKenzie, Marie Waltz, Karen Hauck, Elliot Chiprut, David Roberts, Jon Chivetta, Jane Winner, Marilyn Romain, Elly Evans, Diane Hall, Denise Sutton, Sally Steinberg, Elsie Wanjohi, Mary Jo and Bill Bezdek, and most especially my brother, Robert Romer.

Finally, I would like to express my gratitude to Betty Leaver, Managing Editor of MSI Press, for coming up with the concept for this book and for all the encouragement she has given me the past two years.

Thank you, all!

Contents

Introduction:
Learning To Be Alone

When we lose a loved one—a friend or relative—our first reaction, after pain, is usually atavistic: how will this affect me? When we lose a spouse, however, no such reaction is possible. The grieving widower or widow soon becomes aware that this loss is catastrophic in a different way: it's more like losing a part of oneself, one's arms or legs. We keep waiting for that dear one to reappear; we want to claim him or her—until we realize this isn't going to happen. We're alone. Not only are we in pain, but also we're alone.

For the widower in particular, this can be quite a shock. Accustomed to having a "right hand" or equal partner around, the newly bereaved man can be thrown into confusion. He had probably not realized his level of co-dependency. Suddenly, he is facing life without his spouse in a thousand different ways, and he is devastated.

What can you do when your beloved wife dies? As one of the widowers in this book stated, acceptance is the key. You have to accept the reality that your spouse is gone and that you must continue your life's journey without her. Nothing can bring your dear wife back, but there are ways to comfort yourself. Other men have figured it out, and so can you. There are numerous paths you can take to rebuild your life, from learning how to live by yourself to deciding to remarry. The men interviewed in this book have shared their stories in the hope that what they've gone through will help you, the new widower, cope with your loss.

God bless you as you put the pieces of your life back together!

Part One: Grieving

Chapter One

Rick Bernhard

"Don't try to fill that set of shoes. Keep busy!"

"Marti was a Southern girl. I grew up on the South Shore of Long Island. Other women wanted to know how much you were making, but not Marti," said Rick Bernhard, an attractive 50-year old widower who still mourns his wife after five years.

"We met at the Corvette Lounge in St. Cloud, Florida. She didn't like me at first—I was in my New York mentality," Rick told me.

Nonetheless, the two hit it off. Both liked NASCAR and boats. Rick was working for the Flanagan Association as a consultant, getting seed money for developing Assisted Living Facilities. After their first meeting, Rick and Marti didn't see each other for ten days. "I was at a boat race. You can't take women to a boat race; they distract you," Rick said. "Marti didn't understand this at first, but I explained."

After the boat race, they got together again. "We fell for each other. Marti was never judgmental. She was brilliant, good in bed. Socially, she could handle herself."

The two got married in 1999. Marti's dream was to become an airline dispatcher, and Rick put her through school. Once she got her license, Rick followed her to Atlanta so she could work for Delta.

"She did ten-hour shifts," Rick recalled. "Nobody knows about dispatchers. She shared Operation Control with a pilot."

Rick and Marti were ecstatically happy for a while. Love notes from the time read: "Richard, I love you with all my soul. You have brought so much to my life. Thank you for loving me, M," and "Baby, I love you and will miss you all day. Turn my phone on and bring it, please. Be careful. Your husband, Richard."

Then, tragedy struck—lung cancer. "They didn't tell me what was going on," Rick said.

Marti underwent chemotherapy. "The chemo wore her down. It wears you down mentally, and then you go."

Rick and Marti left Atlanta and moved back to St. Cloud so Marti could be near her family, but it was too late. On October 3, 2008, Marti died.

****

Rick had a lot of trouble coming to grips with his loss. "I cried a lot," he recalls. "I went to bars and drank. I was living across the street from the Altamonte mall so I didn't have to drive."

Then, one day he did get a DUI. It turned out to be a blessing in disguise.

"The therapy in the DUI school helped me," he said. "If I hadn't had that, I would have been in real trouble. The people at the DUI school fell in love with me when they found out I'd just lost my wife."

It was at DUI school that Rick learned about the five stages of grief (denial, anger, bargaining, depression and acceptance—more on these later). He had pushed everyone away, even his parents at first. "My parents had a lot going on," Rick said. "My sister Linda had just gotten sick at the same time."

As he began to come back to life, Rick was faced with the task of closing out Marti's estate. "Marti never made a will, because that would have made it clear she was dying," he explained.

Every day there were hours of phone calls. He was still doing consulting and going to the bar for comfort. "That, and the DUI classes—an odd mix," he admits.

It took him a couple of years to have any contact with women. In 2010, he finally came out of his shell. "Two women helped me," he said. "Kathy, a friend of Marti's—we'd spend time together, and Melanie, Marti's adopted daughter—actually, just a friend. Talking and listening—I still talk to Melanie all the time."

Rick said Melanie and he started having sex at one point, but she was "too wild for me." These two women, as well as his parents, got Rick through the worst of his grieving. There were, however, other problems. Rick, along with Marti's mother, had gone through $80,000 trying to fight Marti's cancer. It took two years, but Rick's house was finally foreclosed. "It was a nightmare," he recalled. "I was doing consulting work, living off food stamps, selling everything at yard sales. The more I got rid of, the better I felt. I donated her clothes to a woman's shelter."

He remembers the first holiday being hard. "I flew up to North Carolina to be with my parents. Being around them at the holidays was good." Then, his sister Linda died in 2012, and that brought it all back.

****

"I take Marti's ashes with me," Rick said. "I have a little stainless steel canister—I'll put a little under a plant."

Rick prays for Marti and for his sister Linda. "I pray my own little prayer. I don't go to Church. When I see these guys on TV praying about money, it sickens me. I pray Marti has the love and warmth of God."

"You could have no money, but if you have love it doesn't matter," Rick said. "What I had was real."

He says that now, at this point in his life, the only thing he's mad about is that he didn't get Marti to the doctor sooner. "She used to drive me crazy with the smoking," he said. "She would not go to the doctor. It's the only thing we argued about. I could hear her coughing out on the porch.

"I did everything I could. My guilt was I didn't start sooner, but she died with grace and dignity."

Rick is comforted by the fact that he and his wife had unconditional love. "We were married for nine years, but we were married forever," he said. "It was that kind of love."

"She was my True North."

****

Rick's Advice for Widowers:

"Get rid of the stuff. Get out of the house. Don't make any decisions the first year of mourning."

"Don't try to fill that set of shoes. Keep busy."

Guidelines for Widowers

1. Rick found comfort in learning about the five stages of grief. For some people, knowing that what they're going through is to be expected can be a great relief.

2. Therapy, in whatever form (Rick got his from a DUI course), can also be tremendously helpful.

3. Try to spend your first holiday with loved ones. If that's not possible, go out and do something—don't stay home alone (see the chapter on Holidays).

4. Engage in whatever ritual brings you solace—Rick took Marti's ashes with him, scattering them a little at a time.

5. Remember the unconditional love you had with your spouse—the depth of your love is comfort in itself.

Chapter Two

Rituals

As a widower, you have joined a special group of individuals who bear a unique type of pain. Not only are you dealing with the loss of a loved one, you are also handling a changing identity, an identity you may have carried with you for 10, 20, or 40 years—that of a husband. Suddenly you're a single person again, but it's not at all like being single in your 20s or 30s. Now you probably find yourself unsure about this status, maybe even a bit embarrassed. "Single?" you ask. "Who, me?"

In actual fact, your consciousness is still married. You may be alone physically, but in your head you're still trying to communicate with the woman you've known for so many years. You're used to doing that, right? Checking things out with the wife?

So your identity, your self-image, has become a bit blurred. You look in the mirror, and the face you see is somewhat unfamiliar. Who is that worried looking guy with the blood-shot eyes? You find yourself having trouble making simple decisions—what to have for dinner, for instance, or where to spend your Saturday afternoon. You and your wife had a little ritual for Saturday—not every Saturday, but often enough: you'd go out for lunch, then head over to the Home Depot (for you) and TJ Maxx (for her). They were both at the same shopping mall, next door to each other, in fact. It was nice taking your time examining the tools, not having to rush because you knew your wife was taking her time next door, looking around and trying on stuff for an hour or so.

Well, think about it: you can still do both of those things. Sure, lunch will not be as cozy without your spouse, but maybe you can arrange to meet a friend. As for going to the Home Depot—you were in that store by yourself, dear man! You can certainly maintain this ritual (and others like it) with just a little effort.

And you should. Even though your weekly trip to the Farmer's Market and Thursday night bowling won't be the same without your wife, you need to continue those activities and others like them, in order to maintain your identity. You chose those activities because they suited you, and they still do.

Did you enjoy making a big breakfast on Sunday morning? Continue to do so. If necessary, invite a neighbor to enjoy it with you. But even if there's no neighbor available, why should you deprive yourself of those pancakes and sausages and of the grapefruit you always prepared so carefully with a touch of cinnamon sugar? You didn't consider yourself a cook any other day of the week, but on Sunday morning, you became Emeril—it was who you are.

You're still that person, and it's a mistake to deny that. Did the two of you run a mile (or two, or three) together on the weekends? Did you go to the movies on Friday night? You need to continue these rituals, even if they're a bit painful at first. Don't stop engaging in the pleasures of life, no matter how much they remind you of your late wife. After a while, the memory will get sweeter and become part of the reason "that thing you do" is so you.

Chapter Three

Learning to Grieve

Grieving is mostly a private matter, and only you know when and how you need to grieve. But, grieve you should—don't try to hold it in, or deny that you feel sad, hurt or lonely. With only one or two exceptions, all of the widowers I spoke with shed some tears as we talked. If they were emotional enough to get teary eyed in front of someone they'd just met, chances are that, alone, they allowed themselves to cry.

And so should you. You need to acknowledge that you miss your loved one, and tears often accompany that acknowledgement. So, don't hold in your tears. This is one situation where it is manly to cry.

How else can you grieve for your late wife effectively? Certainly by talking to friends and relatives about her—do that as much as possible. You can also write about her (one widower I know wrote a short story about his late wife; others have written poems). You can listen to music the two of you enjoyed and visit places you used to go together. Yes, this might be hard at first, and if you need to take someone with you, by all means do so.

According to Dr. Elizabeth Kubler-Ross, the famous Swiss-American psychiatrist who wrote about death and dying, the five stages of grief are denial, anger, bargaining, depression and acceptance. As you can see, we go through several phases before we completely accept the fact that our spouse has died. Most people will take weeks or months to admit to themselves that their loved one has left them; this stage eventually gives way to anger. Bargaining usually takes the form of "If I'd only done this…" and such—depression can follow, or accompany, this phase. Complete acceptance can take years, but after all, there is no hurry. Don't be reluctant to explore these stages thoroughly—if necessary, see a therapist to help you in your grieving process.

Love has a way of healing all wounds, and the more love you can express and receive with friends, relatives and even yourself, the more effective your grieving will be and the more complete your eventual healing.

****

Chapter Four

Holidays

Where do you go to celebrate a holiday without your wife? Perhaps you don't want to celebrate at all—maybe you'd rather put your head under a pillow and wait until all the hoopla is over.

But you can't. If you have children (or parents), they'll probably want to spend the holiday with you, if for nothing else, to make sure you're all right. But how can you be all right when your heart is broken? The holidays, in particular, will tend to bring out heartache—unless you take steps to keep that from happening.

What kind of steps can you take? If you're a brand new widower, it is probably best to confess your sadness to your daughter, son-in-law, sister, or whichever relative or friend has invited you over. Just say, "I don't feel much like celebrating—do you mind if I go lie down?"

Once in your room, you might want to write a letter to your late wife, wishing her a Merry Christmas or Happy Thanksgiving, and telling her how much you miss her. You can play some music, and yes, you can cry—no one is going to hold it against you. Grieving on a holiday is par for the course for a new widower—just remember to be thankful for the loved ones you still have around you (and then go join them for dinner).

If you're alone, the challenge may be greater. If at all possible, try to go out—eating dinner in a festive restaurant on New Year's Eve will certainly be better than sitting home alone. Order a drink or a glass of wine, smile at the waitress and try to say something nice to her. Your heart will be lifted.

If your first holiday alone is in the spring or summer—your birthday perhaps—the best remedy may be to venture out into nature. Take a walk, go fishing, or do a few laps in a swimming pool. Nature, combined with a little exercise, can do wonders for your saddened heart.

Holidays can be difficult, but they will definitely get easier as time progresses. A holiday is not a normal day, and it does not reflect your degree of coping with bereavement. Don't beat yourself up about feeling bad.

It wouldn't hurt to buy yourself a little present too, no matter what the occasion!

Chapter Five

Bob Murray

"Get out with friends as soon as possible."

"Her name was Jane. I could talk forever about her. She was the heart of the family."

Bob Murray's eyes clouded as he talked about his beloved wife who died in 2009. Bob is a handsome man, whose lively demeanor belies his 86 years.

"I married her right out of high school," Bob told me. "She was 18 years old. We started a family—had four boys."

Their family moved to the country outside Pittsburgh and renovated a 150-year old abandoned house. The husband and wife were both in real estate—Bob as a real estate developer and Jane in residential sales. "As a wife, mother and working woman, she was right at the top," Bob told me. They moved around a lot as Bob's responsibilities increased, but after a number of years, they lost a son.

"He was 35 years old," Bob said. "I quit work, and we moved away. That was 26 years ago." Over the next few years they also lost two grandchildren, which added extra stress to the couple.

Jane became ill around 2004. She had emphysema and also neck problems. "I was her caregiver for five years," Bob said. "The last few years of her life were hard, but she never complained."

Bob told me that after his wife died, he became a recluse at first. "It was very difficult for me. I was not handling it right. I tried to go to some counseling sessions—but I never went back to the same one twice. It was group therapy, too hard for me."

Bob was besieged with loneliness. His only comfort at that time was watching sporting events on TV. "For the period of the game I would forget about everything. That first year and a half you really want to die," he said.

He became more and more depressed, even making one attempt at suicide. "I had a couple of drinks and went out to the garage. I got in the car and turned it on. I thought I'd just fall asleep, but I didn't. After ten minutes I got out and shut off the motor. I was really hoping that I wouldn't wake up."

****

After that, Bob began to realize he was going to have to do something to get himself out of his depression. Even though he was no longer playing golf—he and his wife had been avid golfers before she got sick—he began hanging out at his Club a bit more. He started meeting some other widowers for dinner—they sat at the bar and talked. "We talked about what we were doing. One or two had met other women, and we talked about that.

"Everyone at the Club knew us and would come over and chat with us. I should have tried this earlier—it was better than the counseling sessions."

The men he was socializing with were already friends. Three were widowers, one was divorced. "It was like starting all over again. I started eating better too—prior to that it was just Marie Callender's frozen dinners."

He was at the Club one night when he got a call from a woman named Dori. "My sister had mentioned she'd told this friend of hers, 'Would you please give Bobby a call?' We chatted a while, and I said, 'Why don't I take you out to dinner?' We went to the Malibu Grill—and we've had a great relationship ever since. I go to her house once a week for dinner, and I take her out two or three times a week. She got me going to night clubs and things—she got me back to golf."

It was Dori who also helped Bob with prayer. "I prayed an awful lot when my wife was ill," he said. "I pray a lot and also doubt a lot. Dori had me meet her priest—we got together socially. Talking to the priest helped me. I had my doubts about the future—I can't totally convince myself, but I'm trying."

****

Bob still lives in the same house he shared with his late wife. "I have her ashes in the bedroom," he told me. "The last rose I picked for her—it's still there in a little bottle. The petals are all there. I have it by her ashes.

"Dori says, 'One day at a time.' She keeps repeating that to me."

Bob did not touch his wife's closet until after about a year of going with Dori. Then, a daughter-in-law asked if she could help with the closet. "She bagged everything and took it to Hospice and the churches," Bob recalls. "I would drive the car and help her unload, but she did everything."

Bob told me the only thing left were his wife's shoes—then, about a week before I spoke with him, AmVets called and said they were badly in need of shoes. "I did it myself—three bags of shoes," he said. "AmVets sent me a nice note. Just about everything is gone now.

"It makes you feel a little better—knowing somebody is going to get some use out of it."

Bob said he misses his wife every day. "I took care of her for five years—she took care of me for 55," he said.

Bob's Advice for Widowers

"I think the only thing that I can say is—get out with friends as soon as possible."

Guidelines for Widowers

1. Allow yourself time to "hang out" at places where you feel comfortable and can be with other people. A club, a sports bar, a ball park—you don't necessarily have to do anything, just be there, look around and talk to people a little.

2. Watching sporting events on TV can be a good form of therapy in the early days of grieving. If you're like Bob, you'll find that you can forget about everything else during the period of the game.

3. Bob found that getting together with a group of other single males—widowers and divorced men—brought him tremendous comfort. Try meeting once a week for dinner or a drink.

4. Knowing somebody is going to get some good use out of your wife's clothes will make you feel better about cleaning out her closet and drawers.

5. Bob's friend Dori told him, "One day at a time"—good advice for any widower!

Chapter Six

Self-Esteem

What gives you self-esteem? Is it wearing a clean shirt and well-polished shoes when you're heading out to dinner with a friend, whether male or female? Is it the knowledge that you can still be useful as you fix your neighbor's lawn mower, or maybe even her computer?

Is it the fact that the woman in the grocery store smiled at you when you let her go ahead of you in line, or the realization that you can still beat your old pal Phil on the tennis court after 31 years?

All of these things (and more) can contribute to self-esteem, a very useful commodity for a widower to have. Chances are, if you've lost your wife recently, your self-esteem has taken a beating. When our typical routine is drastically altered and we find ourselves struggling with everyday events, one of the first things to plummet is our opinion of ourselves. That good opinion, that high self-regard, is very important in the process of healing.

Most of us are pretty critical of ourselves at all times anyway, but for a widower, self-criticism can border on self-abuse. ("Oh, I can't do anything right without Mary around," or "How come this soup tastes so awful?—I am the world's worst cook!")

You may have married a superwoman—many widowers become convinced of this after their wife's passing—but chances are it's you who is placing way too much blame on yourself. So what if you can't cook? You'll learn to fix your own meals eventually—and you'll learn to clean the house, balance the checkbook, plant the flowers and do all those things your wife accomplished effortlessly. Give it time.

In the meantime, it's important to make special efforts to rebuild the self-esteem that has been displaced since your wife's death. You do this, first of all, by speaking gently to yourself instead of cursing your supposed incompetence. Congratulate yourself for every single good thing you accomplish that you never have before. ("Voila! It's the best chili I ever tasted!" "Wow, I sent birthday cards to all the grandchildren, just like Virginia always did!")

Take special care with your appearance. Now is the time to go out and buy some new clothes, get a haircut, and lose a few pounds. You will be amazed at how much a little self-care affects the way you feel about yourself.

Plan a small trip to a relaxing place, buy a new iphone, or even buy a new boat if you can afford it. No, we don't want to make any big changes during the first year of our bereavement, but spending money on something you know you can afford is a great way to make you feel better about yourself.

Rebuilding your self-esteem is critical to the healing process, and you owe it to yourself to take it seriously. Remember, true self-esteem comes from within—when our thoughts are in harmony with God and nature. Strive to be at peace, and that serenity will give you comfort throughout your day.

Chapter Seven

Cleaning the Closet

Of all the difficult tasks faced by widowers, cleaning out your wife's closet is probably at the top of your list. To be sure, not everyone has this problem—some men just open the closet door, stuff everything in plastic bags and haul them over to the Goodwill.

However, if you're like most widowers, the thought of cleaning out the closet gives you shivers. You just don't want to do it—at least, not right now.

There is no reason why the closet has to be cleaned out on any kind of time table. Bob Murray waited several years, until his daughter-in-law kindly volunteered to do the task for him. If you have a sister, a daughter or a friend who has volunteered to help with this chore, by all means let them. Cleaning the closet is not a rite-of-passage—it's a task that needs to be taken care of by whomever is willing to do it.

Once Bob's daughter-in-law had sorted out the clothes and given them away, Bob found he had no trouble with his wife's shoes. AmVets had called asking for shoes, and he was happy to help out, feeling grateful that his wife's belongings could be put to good use.

Jack Don, interviewed later in this book, developed his own technique for handling his wife's closet. When kindly neighbors invited him over for coffee or a meal, he would invite them back to his place to take whatever they wanted from his well-stocked closet. (Since everyone knew that his late wife had some very nice clothes, Jack had quite a few takers.) Rick Bernhard found that getting rid of everything as soon as possible made him feel a whole lot better.

However you choose to handle your wife's closet, remember that it's nobody's business but your own. You, and only you, will know when and how to deal with this task—in a way that honors your wife's memory and soothes your heart.

****

Chapter Eight

Venturing Out

As you begin to go out alone—maybe for lunch at an outdoor patio restaurant on a nice day or just to get a beer at a neighborhood tavern—you may feel that other people are looking at you. You're alone. As you look around, it may seem like everyone else is coupled up—you just never noticed it before because you too were part of a couple. Now you're not, and it feels—weird.

Cautiously, sitting out in the sun on the patio, you adjust your shirt collar. It appears to you that all the other patrons are younger than you. Oh well. The waitress approaches, smiling. " I haven't seen you in a while," she exclaims, handing you a menu. "Where's your lovely wife?"

You contemplate getting up and leaving, but you don't. "Well, she, uh—she passed away," you say, not looking at the waitress. "It was kinda sudden."

"Oh, my God!" The waitress claps her hand to her mouth. You realize she's only about 20 years old, around the age of your granddaughter. "I didn't know," the girl continues. "When?"

"Uh, it was about a month ago, I guess." You manage to look up at her, your mouth twisting into a grimace. "I'm okay."

"I am so sorry!" the waitress says sincerely. "I wondered why I hadn't seen you in a while. You two were our favorite customers— and you still are, of course," she continues. "Let me get you something to drink—what would you like?"

"Just coffee," you say, relieved the conversation is over. The waitress scurries off, and you begin to relax.

Then something funny happens—it's like a weight starts to lift off your shoulders. You survived the encounter, but more than that—you feel rather comfortable sitting here in the sunshine, waiting for your coffee. And didn't the waitress say that you still are one of her favorite customers?

You lean back in your chair and reach for the menu lying on the corner of the table. The Reuben sandwich catches your eye and your mouth waters. Suddenly—for the first time in a month—you're hungry.

The waitress approaches with your coffee. "Here you are," she says, carefully placing the coffee in front of you. "And I brought you extra sugar because I know you like it that way."

"Thanks. I'll have the Reuben please," you say, smiling.

Part Two: Consoling Yourself

Chapter Nine

Dennis Hansen

"My daughter saved me. I could have given up on life if I didn't have that little six-year old..."

Dennis Hansen's daughter, Monique, was just three years old when Hospice came in to care for Kety, her mother. Kety had been battling cancer for seven years at that point, and she and Dennis kept up the fight for three more years after that, until Kety passed on in 2005.

"Kety was a Christian lady, very loving," Dennis said of his late wife. "She was from Equador. We met in Miami in 1990, the year we were married."

The end of Kety's battle was rough for both Dennis and his daughter. "She had liver and bone cancer, very painful," Dennis told me. "They called it breast cancer that had spread to her liver."

Dennis recalled how he had returned home one day to find his house surrounded by fire trucks, police cars and ambulances.

"Kety had lost control of her pain," he said. "It took six paramedics to get her into an ambulance, and 12 hours before they could control her pain.

"But she never lost her faith, not like me. She was faithful to the end. That little lady was the toughest person I have ever known."

Dennis told me that after Kety passed on, his own faith in God disappeared. "If there was a god, I wanted nothing to do with him—anyone who would allow her to go through that.

"I wanted to have war with God," he said. "I challenged Him to come down and take me on."

Dennis went into a depression after Kety's death. He was working at home as a commercial artist, and sometimes he could barely even work, but he had to keep things going for the sake of his daughter, Monique.

"My daughter never saw me cry," he said. "I got her involved in all sorts of things to keep her busy. I got her a puppy before her mom passed away. I got her into girl scouts. I got her into soccer, and she's still very involved in that."

"It's a real busy deal to be a soccer dad," he said.

Dennis told me that Monique doesn't talk about her mother too much. It has been eight years since Kety passed on, and Monique is about to start high school. "Children are very resilient," he said. "She doesn't remember too much about her mom."

****

Dennis found that his own struggle with depression was harder to handle. He felt some guilt and had trouble understanding why someone as good as Kety had passed on so young. "She was a lot better person than me, yet I'm still here," he said.

He had stopped going to church three months after his wife passed on—the church he and Kety had attended during their marriage. "I was doubting my faith. I couldn't continue," he said.

But he had one glimmer of hope. A chaplain from Hospice had told him, "Maybe you are where God wants you to be right now." The idea stayed with him, and as the years went by, he again began to believe there might be a God. He had started "power walking," and, on his walks, he began to pray.

"It was my alone-time," he said. "I walk any chance I get. They say God speaks to everyone, but I'd been too enraged to listen."

On his walks, which were usually taken out in farmlands, he began to notice things. "You see stuff you never see driving," he told me. "Trees, unusual animals—Native Americans have a term for it when you see something out of the ordinary, like a doe and her fawn in the daytime. They call it 'Good Medicine.' It's a sign from the Creator."

Dennis said that his walks in nature began to stimulate his neglected love of painting. His favorite medium is watercolor. "I've been an artist since 1978. I'm almost 53—I feel like I'm a hundred."

"I believe my daughter saved me," he said. "I could have given up on life if I didn't have that little six-year old. I needed a reason to be here. Someday she may understand."

****

Another consolation came into Dennis's life recently, which he considers almost a miracle.

"This year, I was able to get in touch with my first wife, Edith. We were married six years. She lives in Miami, in the same house that we had. She's been through relationships but never remarried."

Dennis explained that he'd written Edith a letter, and she'd called back the same day she got it. "I was grateful to hear from her—after all these years God is restoring a relationship! Just to be friends makes me feel so good," he told me.

Dennis said that recently he and Edith met in Vero Beach—he drove two hours to be there, and she drove three.

"We met—that's the greatest thing that's happened to me in years, besides believing in God again," he said. "I'm just thankful to have her in my life. It confirmed to me that God was always there."

Dennis said that his attitude now is very different from when he and Edith were married. "We're all here to bless each other," he said. "I'm trying not to expect anything. If you have no expectations then everything becomes a blessing."

Dennis's recovered faith is helping him in his delicate job of acting as a single father. He is taking his daughter to The Journey, a contemporary Baptist Church. "She wants to go to college, and I have the first two years paid for," he said. "I'll do whatever it takes.

"My mission in life is to raise my daughter properly."

Dennis's Advice for Widowers

"Don't give up; don't lose hope."
"Learn to trust God in everything."

Guidelines for Widowers

1. Dennis was resurrected from extreme grief when he recovered his faith in God. Finding something to believe in will help you recover your balance and aid in your healing process.

2. Intense physical exercise, such as "power walking," can get you out of your head and into life again (see the chapter on Exercise).

3. If you have a young child to care for, be grateful for that gift. Dennis found his daughter Monique to be a lifesaver for him and his grief.

4. Get involved in your child's activities. Dennis became a "soccer dad" —attending his daughter's soccer matches and cheering her on. He found that doing something for a person you love was one way to connect with your own sense of loving-kindness.

5. Look up old friends and loved ones whom you haven't seen in a while—even former significant others. Being close with someone you once held dear can be a welcome consolation!

Chapter Ten

Prayer

Most of the widowers I spoke with were familiar with prayer and used it in their grieving process. Prayer comforted Rick Bernhard—"my own little prayer," as he put it. He prayed asking that his late wife Marti had the love and warmth of God. Rick did not consider himself a religious person, but his prayers for his beloved wife were a way for him to stay connected to her.

Dennis Hansen began to pray during his power walks. "It was my alone-time," he said. "God speaks to everyone."

Dear widower, if you have not tried prayer as a way of coming to grips with your loss yet, perhaps now is the time to start. People often turn to prayer "as a last resort," but, judging by its effectiveness with the widowers I spoke to, maybe it should be a first resort. If you're not accustomed to prayer, bear in mind that the practice can be as simple and straight forward as you care to make it. Listening to music, sailing, or even reading a book can offer you the quiet time needed to relinquish your worries and dwell in the comforting arms of God.

Do you like to fish? Few activities are more conducive to prayer than the solitude of a fishing hole, lake or river with a line looped gracefully over the banks of the water. You're alone with your thoughts and the beauty of your memories.

The best prayer is one of gratitude. As a new widower, you may wonder what on earth you have to be grateful for. Look at it this way: you were married to a wonderful woman for 10, 25, maybe 50 years. "As a wife, mother, working woman, she was right at the top," Bob Murray said of his late wife. If you're feeling the same way about your wife, isn't that in itself something to be grateful for? Prayer shows us what we already have and who we are. It lets us realize that we can't let how we feel at any particular moment determine how we view ourselves.

How should we pray? The 23rd Psalm is found to be comforting when dealing with death:

> The Lord is my shepherd; I shall not want.
>
> He maketh me to lie down in green pastures: he leadeth me beside the still waters.
>
> He restoreth my soul... he leadeth me in the paths of righteousness for his name's sake.
>
> Yea, though I walk through the valley of the shadow of death, I will fear no evil: for thou art with me; thy rod and thy staff they comfort me.
>
> Thou preparest a table before me in the presence of mine enemies:
>
> Thou anointest my head with oil; my cup runneth over.
>
> Surely goodness and mercy shall follow me all the days of my life;
>
> And I will dwell in the house of the Lord for ever.
>
> (Psalm 23: 1-6)

The Lord's Prayer also works well for Christians, and it's easy to remember:

Our Father which art in heaven, Hallowed by thy name.

Thy kingdom come. Thy will be done on earth as it is in heaven.

Give us this day our daily bread. And forgive us our debts, as we forgive our debtors.

And lead us not into temptation, but deliver us from evil:

For thine is the kingdom, and the power, and glory, for ever. Amen.

(Matt. 6:9-12)

Other prayers include the Jabez Prayer, the Serenity Prayer, and the 91st Psalm. Bear in mind that you do not need a formal prayer. Simply asking God to take care of your wife is prayer enough.

And do not forget one of the most effective prayers (and one of the most often answered):

"Dear God, help me!"

God loves you, dear widower. He will always respond to your plea.

****

Chapter Eleven

Do Something for Someone Else

In the movie "About Schmidt," starring Jack Nicholson, Schmidt is a new widower who finds himself at a loss after his wife's death. His only contact seems to be the weekly letter he writes to his sponsored "godchild" Ngandu, a six-year old boy in Tanzania. Schmidt is having trouble adjusting—his house is a mess, and even his own daughter discourages him from making a long visit (although she does allow him to attend her wedding and partially pay for it.)

Coming home from the wedding, which was several states away from where he lived, Schmidt feels his life has no meaning—until he opens a letter from a nun in Tanzania. The Sister tells him how much his letters have meant to Ngandu—enclosed with her letter is a painting by his "godchild," a picture of a grown man and a little boy holding hands. Schmidt's eyes fill with tears as he realizes that, to one person at least, his life has had a great deal of meaning.

If you're like Schmidt and feel your life has no meaning now that you've lost your wife (many widowers do feel this way), you might want to look around and see what you can do to help someone else. It may be as simple as donating your wife's clothes to a worthy organization—Bob Murray found that giving his wife's shoes to AmVets helped him, as he realized the items were going to be used by someone else who really needed them. It may be more complex—Dennis Hansen made it his mission in life to care for his daughter Monique. "She wants to go to college, and I have the first two years paid for," he said. "I'll do whatever it takes."

These widowers found that doing something for someone else helped them get out of their grief for a while and provided a distraction from their worries. Even just picking up the phone and calling another person who might be lonely will provide you with a release from the obsession of your own thoughts, which may not be too pleasant at times.

If your meaning in life has been tied up with helping and pleasing your spouse, you're probably feeling a void now that she's gone. Nothing can replace her, but, like Schmidt, you may find that doing something for someone else can bring a new and welcome purpose back into your world.

Chapter Twelve

Be Nice to Yourself

Are you treating yourself well, dear man? It's important to do so—remember, you've undergone a trauma. As the shock subsides, man has a tendency, sometimes, to reach for an austere, get-a-grip-on-yourself attitude, no coddling. This is exactly the opposite of what you need right now. In fact, if there is anyone around at the moment who will coddle you— a sister, a good friend, maybe one of your children—by all means let that person do so.

If there are no coddlers in sight, I suggest you coddle yourself a bit. It may take some getting used to, but it's exactly what you need. Here are some coddling suggestions:

1. Instead of getting up in the morning and drinking your coffee at the kitchen table, take it outside and sit in the sun. If you live in the city, go to a Starbucks or some other café that serves breakfast in the morning. This little bit of pampering can give you a new perspective on your day.

2. Take yourself shopping. Yes, I know, it's never been your favorite activity—most of your clothes were given to you by your wife on holidays or on your birthday. But since she's no longer around, why not go

to a nice men's store—Joseph A. Banks or the Men's Warehouse— and buy yourself a new pair of pants? After all, you probably need them, don't you?

3. Get tickets to a ballgame—any game. If your town has no team at all, and there are none within traveling distance, stop by the recreation center and catch a Little League game. For the duration of the game, you won't be missing your late wife.

4. Go look at some new cars. The key word here is look. You don't want to make any big decisions the first year of your bereavement, and buying a new car is a big decision, but you can still look, can't you?—And who knows, the universe has a way sometimes of rewarding those who wait.

5. Invite some of the guys over to your house—or host a little gathering at your club or favorite sports bar. It doesn't have to be elaborate—you can serve pizza or take-out ribs at your home—and you can talk, play cards, or watch a sporting event on TV. Bob Murray found that socializing with a few friends was the first thing he did that really picked him up.

6. Take a little trip. If your wife had been ill for a while, you probably haven't gone anywhere of late. Treat yourself to a weekend away from home—just you, on your own. The change of scene will work wonders.

7. Get a massage or spend the day at your favorite gym— but don't stress. This is for relaxation only.

8. Buy yourself a plant. If you've got a green thumb, plant the shrub in your garden; if not, put it by the fireplace or on the kitchen table. Make sure you water it, but not too much!

9. Get a dog. This is not for everyone, certainly, but if you've always wanted one and she didn't…now is the time.

10. Make a list of things you like to do or that you enjoyed doing at different times in your life. Your list can include: watching a wrestling match on TV; taking a walk (or a run) around the block; wearing a baseball cap even though you're not going to a game; having a drink at 5 pm at your favorite bar; calling your children on the weekend; playing hoops with the neighbor's teenage son; making scrambled eggs and bacon for breakfast; making scrambled eggs and bacon for dinner; checking out stuff on the Internet that you usually don't have time for, like who won the Super Bowl in 1982; perusing the aisles of Lowes or Home Depot on Sunday afternoon; watching cooking shows on TV (yes, lots of men do that—really!); making something from a cooking show; swimming laps at the YMCA pool; buying sports equipment; buying electronics; buying musical instruments; watching CNN at 3 in the morning; pruning some trees; watching baseball games all weekend on TV; watching football games all weekend on TV and much, much more.

Do at least one or two things from your list every week—you can do as many as you want.

❄❄❄❄❄❄❄❄❄❄❄❄❄

JOANNA ROMER

Chapter Thirteen

Jack Don

"I have to say in all honesty,
I've learned to be a loner."

Still debonair at 91, Jack Don lives in a penthouse apartment at an upscale senior housing community. His wife Marge passed away in 2008, and he, like many widowers, continues to wear his wedding ring.

"We were married 64 years—her death was a complete surprise to me," Jack said. "We'd been up in Maine at a wedding and got home late. We drove into the garage, she got out of the car and she fell. When I couldn't get her up, I went next door and found my neighbor. We got her inside—she was in distress, and I called 911."

Jack told me he sat with Marge for four hours at the hospital. Finally, the doctor came and informed him that they were going to send her home the next day. The doctor said he thought Jack should get someone to help his wife.

Marge was aware of this conversation, and when Jack kissed her good bye, she whispered, "When you come in the morning, bring my glasses and *The New York Times* crossword puzzle."

Jack went home and got Marge's glasses and the crossword puzzle ready to go—he tightened the screws on the glasses a little because they were loose. He went to bed, but at 1:30 a.m. the phone rang. A man's voice announced, "Are you aware of the fact that your wife is having a heart attack?"

Jack rushed to the hospital, but it was too late. The doctor told him, "I thought she was going to come home, but she didn't make it."

Jack was heartbroken.

****

"My wife and I started going together when she was 16," Jack said. "I have never had a date with anyone else. We were always together. We started having movie dates—you could go to a movie for 25 cents, get a hot dog for 15 cents. We were two kids in a group."

Jack even remembers his first date with Marge: it was June 4, 1938. The two got married five years later, on April 18, 1943.

When Marge died, Jack called both his brother and his life-long friend, Ray—they'd been pals since the 5th grade. Ray came over and stayed with Jack while he made the funeral arrangements—Ray had lost his own wife six or seven months earlier to Alzheimer's disease.

"You don't have a whole lot of time to feel sorry for yourself because there's so much to do," Jack said. "The first three days you spend all your time arranging the funeral. I'm a retired naval officer—I have a small number of family in this area." He notified his relatives in New Jersey. They had a modest funeral, just family and a few close friends.

After that, Jack lived within himself for awhile. He didn't have a lot of ties—he and Marge had moved around a lot;

they'd resided in Hawaii and, before that, California. They were old Navy people who had traveled the world. Jack had been in three wars: World War II, Korea, and Vietnam.

With only a few close friends in the area, Jack found himself getting lonely. He told me he didn't deal with loneliness very well, but he was trying to accept it. "I have to say in all honesty, I've learned to be a loner. I read a lot," he admitted.

One of his other methods for handling loneliness was talking to people on the phone. "A cousin of mine, Frieda, and I have gotten into the habit of a weekly phone conversation," he told me. "About a year ago I called to get her address to send her a Christmas card."

That phone call precipitated their now-weekly chats. Jack said he and Frieda can stretch the same conversation into over an hour. "We repeat the same things over and over," he said in amusement. "I say to myself, 'I'll call Frieda. What am I going to say to her?' She's 84. We talk for an hour at a time. It's somebody to talk to."

Jack has no guilt in connection with his wife's passing, not even survivor's guilt, but he does remember certain incidents that bring a pang to his heart. "I had a perfect wife," he said. "She was a gourmet cook. I can't even fry bacon well." Jack told me Marge graduated second in her high school class. "There was talk she should have been Valedictorian, but this was 1940 and they wanted a boy."

****

Jack didn't have much trouble cleaning out Marge's closet. "Some of our neighbors invited me for coffee, and I kept saying, 'Why don't you come and take a look?' So I gave a lot of [her clothes] away that way."

To console himself, Jack reads poetry and military and political history.

"There's no way I would get married again at 91," Jack told me. "I know a couple of ladies on the West Coast. If I were living out there, I probably would have gotten an attachment to one of them. They are people I've known for years.

"In my adult life I never went to Church," he said. "My wife and I were not actively religious people, but I was having a conversation some years ago with an acquaintance who had lost his wife, and I said, 'If it happened to me, I'd go back to Church. I'd be willing to bet I'd meet a widow who's looking for the same thing I am.

"But when my wife died, I never for an instant thought of looking for another woman. I'm long past the age of sexual needs."

Jack's Advice for Widowers

"I get *The New York Times* every day and read it cover to cover."

Guidelines for Widowers

1. Jack called his long-time friend, Ray, to help him out after his wife died—you may not want to handle everything alone.

2. Talk to people on the phone. Even if you find yourself going over the same information more than once—and you will—phone calls to friends are more than comforting; they are essential. Jack got into the habit of a weekly phone chat with his cousin Frieda, which helped him immensely.

3. When friends and neighbors ask you over for coffee, invite them back to take a look at your late wife's closet. Again, having other people involved in this task helps.

4. Never underestimate the power of a good read. Jack indulges in *The New York Times* every day, and he also reads poetry and military and political history.

5. Wear your wedding ring as long as you want. It will bring you comfort, and you'll know when (and if) you want to move it to another finger.

Chapter Fourteen

Wedding Ring

On the famous television series "Monk," the detective, Adrian Monk, was once questioned about his wedding ring.

"Are you married?" the female pianist asked him.

"No," said Monk. "I'm not."

"But you're wearing a wedding ring!" the woman said in surprise.

"I was married," Monk said. "My wife passed away."

"When was that?" the woman asked.

"Six years ago," Monk answered, as if it were yesterday.

The pianist was silenced; she said no more. Six years is evidently considered a long time for a widower to continue wearing a wedding ring. But is it? Several of the widowers I spoke with still wore rings after three, four, or five years. Who is to say when one has to stop wearing that special sign of love and attachment: the wedding ring.

The wedding ring is a symbol that you have committed yourself to another person for the rest of your life. Not all married men wear a ring, but many do. Some—like Doug Bell (interviewed later in this book)—feel that the marriage vow, "till death do us part," means that when the spouse has passed on, the vow is no longer applicable, while others, such as Jack Don, emphasize the "rest of your life" part. Jack has no plans to remarry, thus he continues to wear his wedding ring. Many widowers feel the same.

If you are like Jack Don or Adrian Monk and still wear a wedding ring, rest assured that it is nobody's business but your own. You may, at some point, slide it onto the third finger on your right hand—or you may not. It's up to you.

After all, there's really only one time when you need to remove the ring you've worn for 20, 30 or 50 years—and that's if and when you decide to marry somebody else.

****

Chapter Fifteen

Friends

If you're having trouble taking care of essential tasks, like paying the bills or settling your wife's estate, should you adopt a macho attitude and tough it out alone? Most of the widowers I spoke to said no—get some help. Sure, you can hire a professional for some of the more difficult jobs (like settling the estate), but you can also ask your friends to assist you with the easier ones. Turning to friends and loved ones for help can take a tremendous burden off your shoulders at a time when you need all your emotional strength to recover from the loss of your wife.

What kind of tasks can friends assist you with? Everything from making funeral arrangements to choosing where to spend your first vacation. Jack Don called upon his life-long friend, Ray, to help him out in the first few weeks. Do you have a pal, a long-time buddy, a close neighbor or a colleague on whom you rely? Someone you know who cares about your well being? Don't be afraid to get on the phone and call that person. Just say, "Hank (or Joe, or Bill), I need some help here. Can you come over and tell me what to do?"

Yes, we like to think we can handle everything, but sometimes we can't. Don't be so hard on yourself. Your long time friend will be honored and happy to help you in your time of need. After all, you'd do the same for him, wouldn't you?

If your long time pal is a woman, it's going to be a whole lot easier—chances are that she has already called to ask what she can do. If the lady is a family friend who is married, you can probably turn as much over to her and her husband as they can handle. You will be blessed in such a situation—just be sure to thank them (both of them) with a special gift as soon as you can think straight.

If the woman in question is unmarried but has been close to you in the past, you'll probably be just as blessed, but you may have to keep a check on your emotions. Remember, you are vulnerable at the moment. Your rescuer may seem like an angel now, but don't promise more in return than you're ready to give. Gratitude is a wonderful trait to cultivate, but you do not necessarily have to pledge life-long fidelity to an individual who merely supplies you with a week's worth of casseroles.

Speaking of casseroles, don't be shy—accepting food from well meaning friends and neighbors is a traditional way for people to help you at this time. All you need do is thank them —and eat it. (Nothing you eat in the early days of your grieving is going to taste like it usually does, but eat it anyway—it is important to maintain your strength.)

As time goes on you may find yourself turning to friends again to fill up the lonesome hours. Several widowers found that calling a friend on the phone was a welcome solace. Be grateful you have such friends; be grateful for your cell phone. Even if you have no idea what you're going to talk about with a particular friend, pick up the phone and call. The dynamics of the phone conversation will bring up subjects you hadn't planned to talk about, such as sports, travel or movies. You will be engaged, and your thoughts will be diverted from your loss.

To get back to the casseroles, those lovely ladies bringing food may also be bringing you solace and companionship in a hundred different ways. (Widower Harry Abbott, whose story appears later in this book, found one such comforter to be more than a friend after a while—he fell in love, and if that happens to you, again, be grateful. God has sent a special person to fill the ache in your heart, and what's wrong with that? Harry waited a while before deciding anything specific. Just because that wonderful woman is your neighbor and is bringing you fried chicken and sweet potato pie, that doesn't mean she isn't a fantastic, incredible human being. If you're feeling something, dear man, go ahead and check it out—just don't make any major decisions —like marriage—before the first year.)

What else can friends do? They can:

- Watch your pets
- Make a difficult phone call for you (such as Social Security or the IRS)
- Help you clean out your wife's closet (ask a woman friend for assistance with this)
- Help you get over the first holiday (just say something to that friend if he or she hasn't brought it up)
- Take you out for a drink, or coffee, at a place you and your wife used to visit, thus breaking the stigma of the location
- Fix you a meal when you just can't seem to get one together
- Sort through papers, photos, keepsakes or anything else that has you stymied

These are just a few of the ways friends can help—if you open yourself up to their love.

Chapter Sixteen

Loneliness

Loneliness can creep up on you even when everything is going fairly well—in fact, sometimes that is exactly when it chooses to confront you: "Think you're okay?" it sneers. "Well, what're you gonna do tonight? It's Saturday night and you're all alone."

Saturday night. Date night. No matter how old we are, the impulse is there to make some kind of a plan—any plan—so you're not spending Saturday night alone. But wait! Didn't you and your wife often stay in on Saturday night? Wasn't that the night you watched the newest release from Netflix, or played card games together while enjoying a big bowl of chili—how about inviting someone over to indulge in something like that? It doesn't have to be another woman (although it can be, if you have such a friend). It can be a neighbor, a buddy, even a relative—let's face it, you're not the only person in the world who is alone on Saturday nights.

If staying home is somehow unbearable to you, put on a nice shirt and go out to a restaurant. Take your sister, or the couple down the street who supplied you with three kinds of homemade soup that first week. Go to a boat show, an auto show, or a home and garden expo—events like that are usually open until 9 p.m. or later, and they offer a great deal of healthy diversions. If no one is available, you can always take in a good movie alone—you'll get absorbed in the film and forget that you're there by yourself.

Get hooked up electronically! Okay, you may not need Twitter just yet, and maybe you've never heard of Instagram—but you can get on Facebook, dear widower. You'll be surprised how many of your old friends from high school and college are already on there, just waiting to hear from you. Why not get an iphone too, so you can get email messages while you travel around town? It will help you beat the widower's blues.

Loneliness drives some widowers to look for companionship fairly early on, and maybe that's just what you need. Bob Murray's spirits were lifted with the advent of Dori—a friend of his sister's who then became his good friend. Whatever it is you need to do to get over loneliness, do it, whether it's hitting the mall on Friday night and buying some sports gear, going to a dance club (if you don't know how to dance—learn!), or joining a social group (look on the Internet for a group that appeals to you). After all, you can still contribute to society in many ways, and the first way to contribute is to heal your own loneliness.

****

Chapter Seventeen

Guerrino Lucas

"If you have a passion for something you enjoy doing, go for it. My passion happened to be dancing."

"Sue was an identical twin. We met at a dance at the Ben Franklin Club in Philadelphia—a private professional club. I was a lousy dancer," said Guerrino Lucas, a charming 76-year old widower who lost his wife in 2011.

Guerrino admits that his dancing ability—like everything else in his life—has changed considerably since Sue's death.

"I was 32 when we got married, and Sue was 25. I had lots of girlfriends prior to that. I just never met the right person until Sue. We got married in 1969."

Guerrino told me that Sue's family was reluctant about the match at first. "Her family was very professional; I came from a blue collar family," he said. "I was a little rough around the edges."

Guerrino went back to school because of Sue's family, taking night courses at Rutgers University and then at Barry

University in Miami later on. "At age 59 I walked across the stage in my cap and gown," he told me.

Guerrino and Sue were married 42 years; they had a daughter, Stacy Ann, and a granddaughter, Avery. Both spouses led active lives until Sue got sick. Guerrino was a real estate developer and Sue was a Parent Educator with The Children's Society. Then, one day, Sue fell down and ended up in the hospital. While there she was diagnosed with the onset of Parkinson's Disease.

Guerrino started noticing changes in her speech patterns, and she developed restless leg syndrome.

"We had to cut the bed in half because she was kicking so much," he said.

But the worst news was Sue's diagnosis as a victim of Lewy Body dementia, the second most common dementia after Alzheimer's. "One of the striking differences [between it] and Alzheimer's is that you know who people are but you lose the ability to communicate with them," Guerrino explained.

Eventually, Sue lost her speech completely. Her body began breaking down—Guerrino brought in Home Health Care, but ultimately had to move his wife to an Assisted Living Facility, and finally, a nursing home.

"She never complained. She always smiled," Guerrino said. "Toward the end she went on a ventilator. And then, boom, everything stopped."

Sue died on September 25, 2011. Her twin sister, Ann, had passed away just a year earlier at age 65.

****

"My guilt was for the inability of Sue to enjoy her grandchild," Guerrino said. "She did get to hold the baby—I took her to the hospital to see her daughter after the birth."

Guerrino said that his two distractions during the first month after Sue's passing were legal work (probate and all that it entails) and his mother, who was 97 and living with him at the time. "Your mind is active when you're taking care of somebody," he said. He also had a small support system with his daughter and grandchild.

He also had prayer. "I go once a week to a prayer group. I'm a Catholic—we have a list of names of people to pray for. I believe in the power of prayer," he said.

Music figured strongly in his life at that time—he has 13,000 songs on his ipod, and he categorizes music into genres such as jazz, swing, and so forth, but it was still difficult being without Sue. His closest friends were all up North. After a year he found himself becoming, as he admits, a couch potato.

"Sitting around the house I was gaining weight," he said. "My blood pressure was going up. Then, one day, about a year ago, I drove by 'Absolutely Ballroom,' a dance studio. I'd seen their sign before. I thought, 'if I can get the nerve, I'll go to the ballroom.'"

It took him a while to go in. "I walked in there one day, the guy was giving a private lesson. He told me they also had group lessons—the next one would be Bolero, a type of Latin dance."

There were about 10 people at the studio when Guerrino showed up for the lesson, a mixture of men and women of all ages. "I got out on the dance floor," he said, "and I could not get it! I came the next lesson and still didn't get it. I hadn't danced in 47 years."

The instructor told Guerrino he might benefit from private lessons. "I started taking private lessons an hour a week. They spoon fed me," he admitted. Eventually he learned the Bolero, Fox Trot, Waltz, Tango, Cha Cha, Swing (East Coast and West Coast), Argentine Tango, Salsa, and several other dances.

"All of a sudden, you start looking forward to it," he told me. "They have live bands at some of the Senior Centers. I'm still learning—that's part of the process.

"I was depressed before—now I'm not."

****

Guerrino said his health has also benefited tremendously in the past year since he started dancing. He has lost weight, his cholesterol has dropped 29 points, and his blood pressure is back to normal. Plus, dancing is said to lower the chance of dementia because it requires thinking and coordination to learn the steps.

"I have developed an email list of 35 people who like to dance," he said. "For instance, there's a sock hop coming up on Saturday —I will email everyone and tell them about it. There's a dance every Friday night at the Italian American Center. You could go dancing every night of the week if you wanted. I like to mix it up: Monday night, Salsa, Tuesday night, Tango..."

He said that often six to eight people will go together to a dance if the event in another city. "Sometimes I'll take one of the gals myself. You start building up your confidence."

Guerrino still misses Sue terribly—for instance, one of his prayer group meetings fell on Valentine's day this past year. "I brought up Sue's name to say a rosary, and I could not finish," he told me. But he is coping, with the help of ballroom dancing, better than he thought he would.

"Sue was a sweet, kind, non-complaining person," he said. "She always had a smile on her face. You just wanted to be with her."

He has no plans to form an attachment with anyone right now. "Some men get married right away just for companionship," he said. "If I get married again, it will be for love."

Guerrino's Advice for Widowers

"If you have a passion for something you enjoy doing, go for it. My passion happened to be dancing and my involvement with my church."

"Reconnect to old friends by attending reunions."

"Dress up, not down. Don't be sloppy in appearance. You will feel better about yourself, and people will notice and compliment you. Especially women."

Guidelines for Widowers

1. Guerrino jumped right in once he got an idea for an activity that would cheer him up. Let your heart lead you to happiness!

2. Whether it's dancing, music, art, woodwork, gardening, or any number of other activities—pouring yourself into an activity as far as you can go will lift your spirits and help you begin healing.

3. Guerrino allowed prayer to become a major part of his life, something that many widowers have discovered brings solace.

4. See if you can find an activity you love that has an added bonus for your health—dancing is certainly one of those activities.

5. Don't forget: caring for another person, such as Guerrino did for his 97 year old mother, can provide you with a gentle distraction from the pain of losing your wife.

Chapter Eighteen

Socializing

Socializing is a bit different than going out with friends, because you can socialize with people who are not your friends—yet.

Widowers who have served as caretakers for their wives may find that, after their spouse has passed on, they've lost touch with friends. Or, like Geurrino Lucas, maybe their close friends from young adulthood are in another city and can only be reached by phone. In such a situation, what can you do to develop new friendships now that you are alone?

The answer is—socialize. The word itself may not be too inviting to some men, conjuring up images of tea parties and mandatory gatherings on behalf of the PTA or some local fundraising effort, but you can socialize for all kinds of reasons, and the benefits for your heart and health are enormous.

Faced with the dilemma of lacking close friends in his current city, Guerrino set about creating his own social network. He followed his passion (a good place to start) and allowed his interest in ballroom dancing to grow into an informal network of both men and women whom he could email about dance events in his community.

Allowing yourself to get involved in ongoing social events, either through your church, your neighborhood or your special interests, such as dancing, can alleviate loneliness and allow you plenty of opportunities to meet new people. Maybe you're not ready to begin dating anyone yet but you'd like to spend some time with members of the opposite sex: attend a church picnic or a neighborhood pot luck at a community center—events such as these will allow you to ease back into the swing of things slowly, without getting you too involved with one specific person.

Socializing is fun, relaxing, and beneficial to the healing process, if done with an open mind and a heart full of friendly camaraderie.

Chapter Nineteen

Learn to Cook

Do you know how to cook? Or are you, like Bob Murray, resorting to Marie Callender's frozen dinners every night? Now, there's nothing wrong with eating frozen dinners. Indeed, they are virtually a life saver when you're tired and hungry and you don't feel like going out.

But, after a while, you may want something a little more... homemade tasting. You're used to your late wife's cooking and wish you could replicate it, but you can't...or can you? If you've never tried cooking, but always wondered what it would be like, now is your chance.

Start with something very, very easy, just one step beyond the frozen dinner category. Most grocery stores have a ready-to-cook section near the meat counter where you can buy such savory items as chicken kabobs with onion and green pepper, meat loaf, and pre-seasoned pork chops. Usually these meals call for 40 to 60 minutes of broiling or baking in a pre-heated oven (make sure you switch the button from pre-heat to bake once you put your entrée in).

How about scrambled eggs? Most everyone has luck with this recipe. Put a little oil in a shallow pan, beat your eggs lightly with salt and pepper, then slide them into the pan.

Watch the eggs carefully to get the right consistency—light, moist scrambled eggs take just a few minutes, so don't over-cook them. You can also warm up a nice slice of ham (also at the meat counter)—sautéed in a little butter, it will be ready in time to go with your eggs. Serve this with a glass of beer, and you've got a great little supper. (Of course scrambled eggs are also wonderful for breakfast, but you knew that.)

Ready to go one step beyond? A simple roast chicken is delicious and quite easy to make. Here's all you do:

1. Buy a whole chicken at the grocery store—three or four pounds is about right and will give you some nice leftovers for a couple of days.

2. Pre-heat your oven to 450 degrees.

3. Prepare your chicken: take the little package of gizzards out of the cavity and set it aside. Rinse the chicken with cold water and pat dry with a paper towel. Peel two cloves of garlic and put them inside the chicken cavity, then tie the legs together with a piece of string.

4. Place the chicken in a shallow roasting pan, and salt and pepper the bird generously.

5. Put the chicken on the center rack in the oven and lower the temperature to 350 degrees right away. Bake 20 minutes to the pound, frequently basting the bird with pan juices during the last half-hour. You can use a large spoon for this or a turkey baster.

Serve the chicken with a little bit of the pan juices, along with potato salad and a frozen vegetable, such as green beans or peas. Voila! You have a wonderful dinner.

Cooking is not hard once you get started, and you may find you enjoy it. You'll certainly enjoy eating your home-cooked meals!

Chapter Twenty

Aging

There have been a number of wonderful movies in recent years focusing on the subject of aging. However, none, in my opinion, capture the glories and possibilities that come with growing older as well as Dustin Hoffman's "Quartet." Set in a beautiful retirement home for musicians in rural England, the film underscores the importance of maintaining one's interests despite aging—in fact, it looks at the process of aging as an opportunity to further celebrate interests until the day we die.

Losing a husband or wife cannot help but remind us of our own mortality, and thus, our age. We have two choices as a bereaved spouse: we can succumb quietly to a second "grave" of permanent mourning, lapsing into darkness until we, too, are no longer of this world, or, we can rejoin the human race, with all its heartaches and complications, joys and triumphs. The widowers who have borne their grief most successfully are those who have latched on to an old interest, or found a new one, to see them through. Jack Don reads poetry and military history, and he devours *The New York Times* from cover to cover every day. What can be more enjoyable than settling down with a cup of coffee and reading—

and let's face it, most of us don't have the time to indulge in this activity until we're older.

As a widower, you may think you have too much time on your hands—but you've always had interests, haven't you? Do you like to garden? Ride a motorcycle? Swim? Turning to an interest or hobby, whether old or new, creates a lifeline to the future—to your future as an active and independent older person.

At the end of the movie "Quartet," the young female doctor talks to the audience that has come to hear the aging opera singers perform. "They inspire us," she says. "Their love of life is infectious and gives us hope for the future." Right now, dear widower, you may not feel capable of inspiring anyone. However, as you become stronger—and you will—you'll realize that the very experience you're going through now will give you wisdom for the future, the type of wisdom that will help others embrace the lives they are living and relish in their own experiences. At times you may feel like your spirit is caught in a prism, where all you see is your own reflection, but actually, your spirit is engaged in the earthly prism of life. We all want to fly into the everlasting, and we will soon enough, but, in the meantime, we can reach that feeling of the everlasting right now, through our imagination, our hobbies and our interests.

You may have lost your wife, but you are still alive. Seize every moment to celebrate your existence—and celebrate you!

Part Three: Starting Over

Chapter Twenty-One

Doug Bell

"Take this seriously: 'Till death do us part.'
You're not meant to stay in grieving."

Doug Bell is a handsome man in his early 60s who is as passionate about life as he was about his late wife. Cheri Bell died on April 13, 2012, just 10 months before I spoke with Doug. She had breast cancer.

"Cheri died early and probably as a result of the medical system," Doug told me. "She had a chemo treatment one day and they said she had a little fluid in her heart. So they gave her diuretics, and, as a result, her kidneys stopped functioning. Why would anyone give her diuretics when she'd just had a chemo treatment?"

Doug and Cheri were married 42 years. They lived on five acres of land in the country, and Doug built their house: "meaning," he says, "I built the house, not a contractor." He had been a mobile radio technician, a position he quit in 2000. After retirement, Doug and Cheri raised animals. They had goats, and Cheri made cheese from the raw milk. "The animals were more her thing than mine," Doug said. "I wanted to do something for her, so that's why we had the goats. I built a pasture for her."

The couple also had dogs. "We did rescue puppies. We always got the dogs that were rejected," Doug told me.

"Cheri was a tough woman. She put up with pain better than most men," he said. "My grieving was because of the way she died. I'm not mad at God. My faith is part of my survival."

****

Within the first couple of months after Cheri's death, Doug bought a guitar. "I had played the guitar before—at one time I had a rock and roll group. I also had a Christian group. When Cheri died, I decided this was the time to get back into it."

Doug's sister Marsha had been playing the piano at a local nursing home—he started going with Marsha to accompany her on guitar. He now plays at the nursing home once a month.

He also plays the music at the home church he attends. "I used to go to a home church and went back to it—Jeff [a friend] is the minister," he said. "It's a group of believers who get together weekly."

After Cheri passed away, Doug's prayer life changed. "When I prayed for Cheri, exhaustively, it was a little disappointing because it didn't work the way I wanted," he said. Now his prayers have turned to a request for acceptance. "I'm not getting mad and saying, 'why?'" Doug told me. "'Thy will be done.' The universe is terminal."

He has given away most of Cheri's clothes, but he still has a few items around. "The things that I thought somebody could get some use out of, I gave to them. I haven't gotten rid of everything. I still have a lot of her stuff but it's not because

I'm hanging onto it—except for some hand-made vests she made, just because she made them."

Doug said he felt heavy-duty loneliness at first. He started going out to Minister Jeff's house and going to visit his sister, Marsha. He went shopping, and, after four months, he made the decision to go on Internet dating sites.

Doug believes that his wife would not have wanted him to sit around and brood. "I went on Christian Mingle and put up a pretty extensive biography. Everyone was divorced, and I'm not sure a divorced person was what I wanted."

Then he went on Zoosk and met Suzie.

* * * * * * * * * * * * * *

"Suzie was a widow about a year," Doug said. "I talked to five girls before I met her. I felt God sorted things out for me—that's the way I think God works."

He gave me an example of what he meant by that. "One of the other girls was an agnostic. We met and had supper, and we laughed—she wanted me to write and tell her what I didn't like about her."

Doug said he thought this was a strange request. As it turned out, he didn't have to undertake that task. "She ultimately wrote me and said, 'Our lifestyles are too different,'" he recalled.

Suzie had also seen a couple of other men before meeting Doug. "She said the men she met were mostly interested in sex, and that's not what she was interested in," Doug told me. He added that he too hadn't wanted any one-night stands. "I felt God brought us together," he said. "I prayed for this."

When Suzie heard from Doug on Zoosk, she tried to write him back but her membership had expired. "She spent $70 to get back on, just so she could write me a letter," Doug said, laughing.

Doug and Suzie ultimately got together and began seeing each other. They hit it off from the beginning, and he remembers one of their early dates fondly. "When we parted, I said, 'Can I give you a kiss?' She told me later it was such a tender kiss."

****

Doug says that having Suzie as a girlfriend is "cathartic."

"I don't do a whole lot of anything now but music and enjoying my girlfriend. I did try to honor the animals Cheri had."

Doug's Advice for Widowers

"The bottom line to me is, find a way to understand and accept the sovereignty of God. Know that life is not the way you expect. Say, 'I'm here, and I don't care if I die tomorrow.' Don't fight Him."

"Take this seriously: 'Till death do us part.' You're not meant to stay in grieving. I don't care about the past. All I care about is today and the future."

"You've got to look forward, and that's what I've been doing."

Guidelines for Widowers

1. Now is the time to resuscitate an old interest or hobby. Doug bought a guitar—a former passionate pursuit—within two month after his wife's passing. Reviving this interest brought him comfort and provided him with an opportunity to serve others through his music.

2. Don't feel you have to get rid of everything of your wife's right away. Doug kept some of Cheri's handmade vests—because she made them.

3. If you feel the need to connect with another person of the opposite sex, Internet dating sites are a great place to start. (See the chapter on Dating.)

4. On the other hand, don't feel compelled to hook up with the first woman you meet. Doug was picky about who he wanted to spend time with—you should be too.

5. Take it easy, even if you don't do anything but enjoy a new creative pursuit (and maybe a new person in your life)—that's enough for the first year.

Chapter Twenty-Two

Dating

How soon should a widower start dating after the death of his wife? The answer, of course, varies from man to man. Some men jump right in; others, like Jack Don, don't feel a need to engage in a dating relationship. "At 91, I'm long past the age of sexual needs," Jack said.

Widower Doug Bell, along with several others, felt that his wife would not want him to sit around and brood. Doug's interpretation of marriage vows—"'Till death do us part"—supported his decision to join two dating sites, which eventually led to a new relationship. Doug felt strongly that, once his spouse had died, he owed it to himself to move forward with his life.

Is a widower being disloyal to the memory of his late wife by engaging in a new relationship, especially an intense, physical relationship? Most widowers say no. Any hesitancy seems to lie more with the individual's inclination, rather than it being a reluctance based on spousal loyalty. If it does get too intense, the widower can always disengage, as Rick Bernhard did. "She was too wild for me," Rick said of a friend he dated (at least at that particular moment in his life).

Several widowers pointed out the plus factors of starting to date within the first year of bereavement. "It was cathartic," Doug Bell said when describing the effects of his new relationship with Suzie. Certainly the comfort and companionship of another human being at this difficult time in your life is a huge bonus. Having somebody to talk to, to share things with, and to go out and enjoy some music or movies with—will certainly ease the loneliness a widower feels at the sudden loss of his wife.

Where can you look for an appropriate dating partner? Internet dating sites attracted more than one widower I spoke with. The most well known are eHarmony, Zoosk, and Match.com. Christian Mingle is a popular site for Christian widowers. The cost of membership on most sites ranges from $20 to $80 per month. The procedure is simple: just log on to the site and follow the directions given. You'll need to post a picture of yourself, along with a biography in most cases, and if you need help with these tasks, ask an Internet savvy friend or relative for assistance. Remember, everyone wants you to progress in your healing, so don't feel uncomfortable asking for help or exposing your need for companionship. It's a natural, normal desire.

If you're a working man, chances are you've already discovered that the workplace includes some pretty nice women, several of whom you may not have noticed before. It's not a crime to ask a co-worker to join you for a cup of coffee or a drink after work (unless your company specifically forbids it). Keep it simple at first—if the two of you get along, you can move on to dinner and dancing, or perhaps a ball game if the lady in question enjoys sports.

Other likely places for a widower to meet women include church, social clubs, or friend's houses. Single men are usually in demand, so if you let your friends and neighbors know that you're open to such experiences, they will probably oblige.

Above all, keep an open mind about your early dating experiences. As Rick Bernhard put it, "Don't try to fill that set of shoes." If you go about comparing every woman you meet with your late wife, you're probably not going to have a very good dating experience. Rather than judging, try to give the woman you're with a good time. That may set the tone for having a good time yourself!

Chapter Twenty-Three

Passionate Pursuits

A passionate pursuit is more than a hobby. It is an interest or activity you pour your soul into—it's so much a part of you that it becomes you, as part of your makeup. You can't really remember a time when you weren't in love with…(music, camping, water skiing, indoor gardening, outdoor gardening, photography, ballroom dancing, motorcycle riding, traveling, tarpon fishing, surfing, or any number of other engaging activities). The point is, this pursuit is more than a pastime for you—it's part of your life.

The only trouble is, as a new widower, you may have neglected your passionate pursuit for a while. Maybe your wife was sick for a long time, and you didn't have a chance to pursue your "second love." Maybe you just didn't have the heart for it. For whatever reason, you haven't been involved in your passionate pursuit for quite some time—months, maybe even years.

Now is the time to resuscitate that worthwhile interest. Doug Bell played the guitar most of his life. At one time he had a rock and roll band, at another, a Christian group. When Doug's wife died, one of the first things he did was to go out and buy himself a guitar. Soon he was playing music for his church, and he was accompanying his sister on musical visits to a nursing home. Involving himself wholeheartedly in something he'd always loved doing was the first step in Doug's healing.

Do you have a passionate pursuit? If so, now is the time to embrace it gladly. For Jack Don, it was reading military history, and for Bob Murray it was golf. (Bob knew he was on the road to healing his grief when his zest for golf came back.) For Dennis Hansen, it was watercolor painting, which he re-discovered while out "power walking," another avid interest.

You can identify a passionate pursuit when the thought of it makes you happy, maybe even a little excited. Even if you're not quite ready to plunge in, there are ways you can stimulate the return of your interest. If you like to paint, go to an art supply store and wander around a bit, looking at paints and canvases. If surfing is your thing, head over to the beach where you can watch the young people do it—maybe you'll feel an urge to compete.

Love is love, and while nothing can replace the love you had for your wife, engaging in your passionate pursuit will give you love—something you could use right about now.

Chapter Twenty-Four

Letting Go

Why would we let go of someone we have been with for most of our life? In a word, because we have to. While we may continue to grieve for our dear wife longer than a year, and will certainly miss her much longer than that, "letting go" is essential for our survival.

What, exactly, are we letting go of, and how do we do it? We are letting go of co-dependency, which tells us that we're not quite "whole" without our late wife. This is actually not true and never was true, but it's part of the romantic mystery of life and love to feel one with the other person, as if our soul is one part of a whole and our mate's soul is the other part. To some people, this is where the idea of soul-mates comes from—two parts of a whole, two sides of a coin.

In actuality, all of us are born as individuals and will pass on that way too. Ideally, in a marriage, we will retain a good portion of our individuality, so that we don't totally identify ourselves with the other person. Widower George Lane (interviewed later in this book) gave some advice to men who might soon be bereaved: "Try to have your own life while you have your life together." Doug Bell's philosophy of taking, "till death do us part," literally, meant letting go not only of his co-dependency, but also of his anger at the way she died.

If you have become co-dependent in your marriage, now is the time when you must let go of that dependency and start to claim your identity as a whole, independent person. Once again, this has nothing to do with how much you loved your late wife—it has more to do with your image of yourself.

How do we go about letting go? It will probably start right away, without you doing anything about it, as you begin to realize that she is not there to talk to, to do things with or to be around. This is painful of course, but it will become easier with time, and it will be more bearable if you begin to engage in activities that you know you like right away. After a while, say six or seven months, you will start to realize that it's okay to enjoy yourself while taking a walk or going out for a beer; it's okay to plan a future; it's even okay to think about being with another person. Or, if the idea of being with someone else is not appealing, you may find yourself starting to feel comfortable on your own, in a way you wouldn't have imagined just a few months earlier.

It may take years to completely let go of your dependency, but there are some signs that you are doing it—moving your wedding ring to your right hand, for instance, or removing it altogether. Perhaps you are starting to feel relaxed in your home again, instead of feeling like you are waiting around for your dear one to appear. Letting go is a subtle process, and it requires patience—it's an act of grace, whereby God grants you what appears to be a second chance at happiness. Whether you embrace this chance after six months or six years, it will come eventually.

Remember, you need not ever let go of your love for your wife. Love is forever.

Chapter Twenty-Five

"Bo" Bowman

"Do the thing you were never able to do when you were married."

"Milly was the leader in our relationship. She was home and I was running around all over the world," said "Bo" Bowman while talking about why he so treasures the memory of his wife.

Bo was in the Navy for 20 years, and he worked with ATT as an engineer for 25 years. To say he misses Milly is an understatement. The two were married for 66 years, and Bo thinks of Milly, who died in 2010, every day of his life.

"She was a trooper," he told me. "I am not myself yet. I still feel like a part of me is missing."

In order to demonstrate his love for Milly, Bo made a cookbook of 100 of her best recipes. "I thought the most appropriate thing I could do was to generate some type of memorial for her," he said. "I gave a copy to all her relatives and most of her friends, and kept one copy for me."

Bo showed me the cookbook, titled: "Milly's Recipes and Memoir." It is a beautifully put together book, with photographs of the dishes and carefully printed recipes. "I typed them all and duplicated them, and constructed the book," Bo said.

- The cookbook is full of comfort food:
- Indian Apple Chicken Salad
- Black Bean Soup
- Quick Monkey Bread
- Sausage Casserole
- Chocolate Almond Apricot Brittle
- Walnut Pie

"I use it all the time," he told me. "I was making fondue last week."

In addition, Milly's picture is on the cover. "I never pick the book up without seeing her," he said. "Everybody loved her," he said. "She worked 50 years teaching pre-school and Sunday school. She was that kind of girl."

Milly had a long illness. "We could see it coming," Bo said.

He told me prayer helped him deal with her passing. "I talked to God—I do that regularly," he said. Both Milly and Bo were active churchgoers, and Bo continues to be active. He was a substitute teacher in the men's Bible class. "When I got to be 80 I thought I'd hang it up," he said, smiling.

But it was the cookbook and all that it entailed that got him through the first few months. "I pushed grief aside," he recalled.

****

In two months, Bo will move to either the Soldiers' and Airmen's Home in Washington, DC or to the Soldiers' and Sailors' Home in Gulfport, MS. He's on the wait list for both.

"For one thing, I will not be alone," he said. "I had a stroke two years ago—last week I fell."

In the Home, he'll always have someone around. "I still have a problem with loneliness—especially at mealtimes," he said.

In order to combat the problem, he joined Weight Watchers. "You're concerned about something besides your feelings," he told me. "It's a distraction. You go to meetings once a week. Every day I have to read the directions—what I should and shouldn't eat to manage my weight."

Bo recommends joining a group—any group—to combat loneliness. He is not interested in romance, but he does advocate socializing with the opposite sex. "I have a lady friend, Dottie; her husband passed away last year. Milly and I were friends with Dottie and her husband for 20 years. She's down here for the winter. We're going to the Little Theater on Saturday to see 'The Drowsy Chaperone.'"

Bo said his family is a tightly knit group. He has a daughter in Washington, DC, whom he'll see more of if he moves to the Soldiers' and Airmen's Home. He's looking forward to that, as well as to the camaraderie of being with people who shared his experiences in the military: "In both the homes, you have to have served in the army, navy or marine corps for 20 years or more." Bo himself was in the Berlin Airlift in 1948.

"I'll never get back to what I was," he told me. "But I'll get to be a whole person again."

Bo's Advice to Widowers

"Do the thing you were never able to do when you were married. In my case, it was flying. Milly didn't like to fly, and, of course, I did. I did it for a living for 20 years. Since she passed, I've flown to Switzerland and Seattle, among other places."

The other activity Bo engages in now is cooking. "Before, Milly did all the cooking," he told me.

Finally, "Keep the lines of communication open. Don't live on an island!"

Guidelines for Widowers

1. Think of some way to honor your wife. Maybe you can continue to tend her favorite flower garden or take care of her pets. Bo went a step beyond in pulling together his wife's recipes and compiling them into a cookbook. It brought him solace, as well as providing an outlet for his creativity.

2. Join a group. Weight Watchers appealed to Bo because he'd been a member before—there were meetings once a week, as well as at-home directives to follow. (Plus, this particular group helped him manage his weight!)

3. If you think you need it, consider moving to a residence where your needs will be looked after. (However, don't make any major decisions—like this one—for the first year of your bereavement.)

4. Even if you're not interested in romance, you can socialize with friends of the opposite sex. An outing or two with a woman friend of your acquaintance can bring a skip to your step.

5. Don't feel bad about following Bo's advice to do things you couldn't do when you were married. Traveling, baseball games, poker nights, and all possibly neglected interests can help with your healing.

Chapter Twenty-Six

Travel

Bo Bowman talked about doing something you couldn't do when you were married as a way of healing yourself. For Bo, that "something" was travel—taking the time to get away from familiar surroundings and go someplace new.

For the new widower, I can think of nothing more beneficial than travel. Jumping in the car or boarding a plane for the sheer purpose of pleasure—when was the last time you did that? If your wife was sick for a while, it's probably been quite some time since you've been anywhere outside your own community. Even if she died suddenly, chances are you stuck pretty close to home for the first few months—grief has a way of incapacitating us, making travel plans next to impossible at first.

But now it's been eight or nine months since her passing, and you're starting to come to yourself. You look around and feel a sudden need to be somewhere else—anywhere but here. Pretty normal, I'd say. You want to get away from your grief, if only for a short time.

You get on the Internet and look up Expedia to see if there are any bargains afoot. Maybe you've got somewhere in mind—maybe it's June, and the Berkshires are beckoning.

Maybe California is calling you, with its memories of a vacation spent in Big Sur with your late wife. It was so lovely then—perhaps that warm sand will take the freeze off of your heart, and perhaps the balmy breezes will blow the cobwebs out of your brain.

You are so right, dear widower. Travel is just what you need right now: a chance to get away from your current state of mourning. When we travel, the everyday activities that seem so crucial to us at home lose some of their urgent necessity. Yes, watering the lawn is important, but the grass can survive on an automatic timer for just one week. (You happen to know, don't you, that rain is predicted for the coming weekend—the weekend you're going south. Hooray!) The same is true for taking care of pets, monitoring the stock market, and your weekly visit to your sister-in-law. These activities can be handled by a caring neighbor, or not at all; your sister-in-law will understand your need to get away from things.

When we travel, we see things differently. Events which have seemed locked in permanence—"I am a retired real estate broker. I had a successful agency for 20 years, and I will never do it again"— suddenly seem to thaw and appear quite differently to you: "I loved doing real estate! Why can't I be a part-time realtor in somebody else's agency for a while?" Sitting by a pool in a lounge chair, and hiking up a mountain trail in the Adirondacks, we begin to realize that we are still alive and that our life has possibilities.

Yes, there's no place like home, but for a new widower, it could be a wise move to do some traveling in order to appreciate everything that's out there. Whatever problems you are feeling in your grief, they will melt in the hot sun as you sit on a beach—even if it's only in Ft. Lauderdale.

Chapter Twenty-Seven

Join a Group

Anyone who has ever been at loose ends and has joined a group for socialization and comfort, knows how rewarding it can be. Groups do more than provide you with something to occupy your time—they give you a purpose for however long you are a member. That purpose is something you, as a new widower, may be sorely needing in your life right now.

Bo Bowman found that joining a local Weight Watchers group provided a welcome distraction as he struggled to put the pieces of his life back together. "You go to meetings once a week," Bo said. "Every day I read the directions…what you should and shouldn't eat." Most groups, no matter what their mission, have specific things that members must do, such as serve as ushers for the monthly community theater presentations, or volunteer to take a youngster to a ballgame as part of the Boys Town responsibilities. Groups provide you with meetings and other things to do on a regular basis—what better way to distract yourself from missing your late wife?

Your choice of a group can be based around a particular interest or hobby, such as the local chess club or boating group. Gardening clubs exist in almost every community, and are not just for women. There are motorcycle clubs (no, not the Hell's Angels—just local guys like you who like to get out for a ride), water skiing groups, tennis clubs and bowling associations. For the more sedentary, look up book clubs or coin collecting groups on the Internet; there are also groups for bird watchers and pet owners. (By the way, if you like animals but don't have a pet yourself, consider volunteering at your local Humane Society. You'll meet a lively group of people with interests similar to your own.) Most big cities will have groups and clubs for every kind of interest imaginable; smaller communities will have more than you'd thought possible. It seems that anytime someone wants to start an organization, there's always another person willing to join them—once you're involved, you're in a group.

Your group does not have to be based on a specific need or interest—it can be purely social. If you have single friends with time on their hands, or friends who are reeling from the death of a spouse or a divorce, call them up and suggest an outing, a fishing trip, or a bowling night. Make it a weekly or monthly event, and suddenly, you've got a group....and you'll have the satisfaction of knowing you're helping your friends as well.

Groups are fun, social, sometimes educational and always distracting. Joining a group is a small step in the direction of healing, but it could become a big step in terms of the satisfaction it will add to your life.

****

Chapter Twenty-Eight

Creativity

We may not think of creativity as a way of handling grief, but several widowers found that embarking upon a creative project was just what was needed. "Bo" Bowman felt that the cookbook he put together of his late wife's recipes not only distracted him and gave him something to think about, but also provided him with a way to pay tribute to his wife, Milly.

"While I was actively pursuing the cookbook, which I knew she'd like, I pushed grief aside," said Bo, explaining just how his creative project helped him to overcome his grief.

Engagement in a creative project of any kind calls for a unique set of circumstances, which, indirectly, can provide a balm for mourning. First, we must decide what our creative project will be. Usually this idea will come to us in a flash, a revelation, so it seems like a gift from God—something to compensate us for our loss. Even if the idea emerges slowly, like cream rising to the surface, once we've tasted its sweetness on our tongue, we're hooked—we know we're going to do it, whatever it is!

After the revelation of the idea comes the planning stage. This may involve making notes, gathering materials or buying something very important to us. For Doug Bell, buying a guitar signaled a return to his real self through the creative act of making music. He'd played the guitar before, but not in a long while; the purchase of the guitar was a significant development in his healing process.

Finally, there's the engagement of the creative act itself. Whether it's art, writing, music, photography or woodwork, "losing yourself" in a creative project may be the step that facilitates your own healing. In the process of creation, you may discover truths not only about your spouse, but about yourself—which is part of the reason the creative process is so valuable to the healing of grief.

We are all creative beings, whether or not we realize it. When we engage in a creative act, we are engaging in a natural process that touches every part of our being, and, inevitably, brings us peace.

Chapter Twenty-Nine

George Lane

*"The community was helping me so much
I didn't have time to think about loneliness."*

George Lane had been a widower just six months at the time of our interview, but he was already well on his way to healing his grief. One of the reasons for this, as George was quick to point out, was the community in which he lived, the Village at Deaton Creek in Hoschton, Georgia, about 40 miles north of Atlanta.

According to George, the community offers a wide range of activities to its over-55 adult population, including fitness training, language lessons, dance instruction and much more. After his beloved wife Catherine died of cancer, George continued the activities they'd enjoyed together, and some that he'd started on his own. He found these pursuits brought him a great deal of comfort.

"I do square dancing on Tuesday night and have Spanish classes in the morning," George told me. "I work out for two hours most every day."

George's wife, Catherine, had been a teacher for much of her life, which may account for George's avid interest in learning new things. After he retired from business in 1999, he and Catherine traveled for 13 years, while also enjoying the leisure activities at Deaton Creek. Their four sons all live in northern Georgia, within driving distance of George's townhouse.

After Catherine's death, on December 20, 2012, George's sons and their wives provided him with loving consolation. "The family was very good," George recalled. "They had me over to their houses numerous times. She [Catherine] had been sick since June, but I was always hoping in my mind that she'd get well."

In addition to his family and the activities he was involved in, George found support among friends and neighbors in the community. "The neighbors invited me over for dinner," he said. "Sometimes they'd invite me over and there would be two or three couples and a single woman."

"It was good to get out of the house—my house has lots of memories, but not all good ones," he added.

George also turned to prayer after his wife's passing. "I was already very active in the Catholic church," he said. "I was an Extraordinary Minister—we help out with the distribution of communion and handle other tasks."

George started going to Mass, and during Lent he went every day. "I let religion be more a part of my life," he said.

George said he was not concerned about guilt after Catherine's passing. "When we prepared our wills 10 or 12 years ago, we said, 'If one passes, the other should go out in the world and continue life.' We had that understanding," he told me.

He admits he felt disappointment that he couldn't help Catherine find a cure for her cancer. "She could see the end coming in November," he said. However, after two or three months he was pretty much back to his old self. "I was missing her," he said. "She was a wonderful woman, but the community was helping so much I didn't have time to sit and think about loneliness."

****

George had lots of help in cleaning out his wife's closet. "I didn't do a thing for six months," he said. "Then my daughters-in-law came over and took a lot of the clothes over to two women who had no money, who were trying to get started in business."

He said that one of his daughters-in-law also packed up some clothing to give away in Guatemala, where she would be traveling the following week. The two women who were entering the business world were also planning to come over and select some more of Catherine's clothes for their use. "I haven't had time to go through her drawers or her books," he said.

He admits that he was very fortunate in another respect as well. "A lady friend of the family lived in the community," he told me. "I got to know Barbara better, and we started doing things together. We've been dating several months."

George and Catherine were married 55 years, and evidently had a wonderful life together. George has let himself be comforted in his grief by his community, his Church, his family and friends, and his many interests. As he himself admits, he is fortunate indeed!

George's Advice for Men Who May Become Widowers

"While you're married, get involved in activities that are specific to you. Try to have your own life while you have your life together."

Guidelines for Widowers

1. While it's true that one of the first rules for widowers is not to make any big changes during the initial year of bereavement, there's always an exception to every rule. If you find yourself living in a depressing place with nothing to do, consider moving to an adult community with activities. It may be just the thing you need to find yourself again.

2. Get involved in your church. Attending church is wonderful, but playing a special role in your church, such as George did, can go even farther in healing your heart.

3. If your friends and neighbors begin to try to "set you up" with single women, go along with them, even if you're not enthusiastic at first. The word will get out that you are open to such invitations, and who knows, you may meet someone interesting who will become a special friend.

4. Comb through old interests you may have had at a different time in your life, and consider taking some brush up lessons—or, start a course of instruction in something completely new.

5. Don't be afraid to do something just for the fun of it. George went square dancing on Tuesday nights and enjoyed it. Nobody wants you to sit around and be miserable.

Chapter Thirty

Get Some Exercise

These days, many men visit gyms regularly or have exercise bikes in their home, but if you don't do anything to stay fit, now is the time to try. Exercise serves a double purpose for a widower. Not only will it help you shed those extra pounds you put on by eating the casseroles and apple pies provided by your neighbors, it will also enable you to get out of your head for a while— this alone makes it worthy of attention.

The tendency of many widowers, after their wife dies, is to withdraw into themselves. Even if you have some very close friends (some men don't have close friends; they have relatives and acquaintances)—you may find yourself preferring not to talk about your bereavement with others. So where do your confused, turbulent emotions go? They swirl around in your head, like a maze you can't get out of no matter how much you want to.

Exercise is a path out of the maze. As you begin to hit a golf ball, jog around the block, or even walk around the block, interesting things will begin to happen to your psyche. Your mind, habituated to repeating, "What am I going to do without her?" or, "If only I'd spent a little more time at home"—is suddenly entertaining new thoughts: "If I get up early I can probably run a mile before I have to get dressed for work." "Boy, I can't believe my backhand is still so good. Looks like I haven't lost my game!" "That landscaping looks good. I never even noticed it before I started taking these walks..."

In other words, as you exercise, your attention is caught by the activity. If you're a golfer, you'll be concentrating on your swing, not missing your late wife's cooking. If you're swimming, you'll be striving to regain your form and endurance—not musing over your wife's form and endurance. As you start to think about yourself, your activities and your strengths in a positive way, life will flow back into you like a balm. Yes, it's helped by endorphins, the hormones released through heavy exercise, but even if you don't do anything strenuous, your outlook will start to change.

Exercise is one of the most important ways we can heal ourselves. So grab your golf clubs, baseball mitt or ping pong paddle (yes, that will work), and get back into your body. You (and it) will feel a whole lot better.

Chapter Thirty-One

Photographs

Almost every widower I spoke with showed me a photograph of his late wife. Sometimes the photos were single framed portraits of the beloved spouse from a year or two before her death; sometimes they were taken much earlier. Often there were composite shots in a large frame: two or three of the couple together, sometimes with their children, combined with one or more of the wife alone. These photographs were always displayed on a living room table or hung on a wall—never hidden away in a back bedroom (although there may have been more photos back there). The point is, these photographs had become a part of the widower's daily life as poignant reminders of a love not lost, but living forever in the widower's memory.

Looking at photographs of a loved one can provide a healthy release of emotion. Bo Bowman put his late wife's picture on the cover of the cookbook he compiled of her recipes. He titled the cookbook, "Milly's Recipes and Memoir," and he told me he looked at Milly's picture every day on the cover. This is a loving way to celebrate a spouse's memory, and your feelings, as time passes, can't help but be healed by it.

If you can think of a way to involve your late wife's photograph in an activity you undertake—a memorial video, or a garden spot with her favorite plants—you will be blessed by your ingenuity. If you're not quite up to this at the moment, just utilize a favorite photo of your wife in some way so that you'll see it daily, such as on a computer screen saver or a bookmark. Either of these will provide unexpected comfort to you as you go about your daily routine.

Photographs have become ubiquitous in the 21st century with the popularity of cell phone cameras, but there will always be one or two pictures—maybe recent or perhaps from long ago, that speak to you in a special way. Treat those photographs with the love and care they deserve: employ them in a way that will remind you, every day, of the wonderful woman you married.

Chapter Thirty-Two

How to Tell When You're Starting to Recover

After nine or ten months (maybe longer), you may begin to notice a subtle shift in your consciousness. The world does not seem so grim, and your heart is starting to feel a bit lighter. Here are some signs that you might be coming out of the fog of grief:

1. You look in the mirror and recognize the face you see as your own, and it doesn't look half bad. Yes, you could use a haircut—but otherwise, that face looks like, well—you.

2. You can sleep through the night without getting up and wandering around your house or apartment wondering where your wife is.

3. The food you make for yourself at home, whether it's breakfast, lunch, or a midnight snack, suddenly tastes good again. Restaurant food may have whet your palette for quite some time, but it's the food you prepare at home that is the real test.

4. You can go to a movie, alone or with a friend, and watch the whole film with enjoyment, and without having your mind wander.

5. You have the urge to get yourself some new clothes (probably something you should have done long ago).

6. You start to notice other women—not necessarily in a lustful way. You may not even be particularly interested in them, but you notice them: what they look like, how they walk—whatever way you noticed women back in the old days.

7. You have a sudden urge to go someplace. It might be going to the West Coast to visit your daughter. It might just be to go out dancing with your next door neighbor. The point is, you want to do something.

8. You take a drastic action. (Not too drastic, however; you don't want to sell your house or get rid of all your stocks just yet!) A moderately risky action is a sign that you're coming back to life: you join a ski club and purchase a new pair of skis; you buy a Harley because you've always wanted one, and you plan a trip to Daytona Beach for Bike Week; you sign up to build houses for Habitat for Humanity, or you decide to go on a mission trip to Haiti with your church. (You know they could use your help, and now you're willing to give it.)

9. You can read a book for at least 30 minutes without losing your concentration (or *The New York Times*, *The Washington Post*, or any news magazine).

10. People are telling you that you look better, and they're no longer bringing you casseroles.

If you can claim any five of these, you are well on the way to recovery. More than five—you may not need the rest of this book. (But keep reading anyway, because it fits in with Item #9.)

Part Four: Your New Life

Chapter Thirty-Three

Harry Abbott

"I didn't go back and forth between, 'Should I get married again or shouldn't I?'—
It was a natural decision…"

Harry Abbot was married to a painter. Bernice painted landscapes in a lovely, primitive style, full of color and a refreshingly innocent perspective. When she passed away on March 17, 2001, Harry had no idea what he would do. The couple had been married 49 years, 11 months. "Bernice always said, 'If I go before you, just put me on an ice flow and send me down the river,'" Harry told me. "She didn't want to be lying around if she wasn't well—Bernice was practical that way."

Harry is an energetic man with salt-and-pepper hair and an engaging smile. He's not the type of person to spend much time courting depression. When Bernice died, Harry turned to the people in his church for help. He also received solace from his children. He has four—Murray, the oldest, who lives in Pittsburgh; Debbie, residing in Reno, Nevada; Elaine, in Lincoln, Nebraska; and Janice, the youngest, who makes her home in DeLand, Florida. "At first I couldn't care less what happened to me," Harry recalled. "I just didn't care—that went on for three months."

Harry told me that right before his wife died, they'd made elaborate plans to commemorate their 50th wedding anniversary. They'd rented several houses in Beach Mountain, North Carolina, where the couple spent their summers, and they were planning to celebrate with all four kids. When Bernice passed away, Harry canceled everything, but the kids wouldn't hear of it. They wanted to celebrate Bernice's life. So the anniversary plans went forward—Harry said it was the beginning of his healing. "We had a dinner and a lunch at the Club. All the kids brought their families—I had six grandchildren. It was wonderful to be together."

After the 50th anniversary celebration, Harry began to "come to." The time spent with his family, and their concern for him, helped to ease the pain of losing his spouse. "I started to feel the gratitude for my wonderful life with Bernice," he told me, adding that there were a number of people in both Beach Mountain and Florida, where Harry and Bernice wintered, who helped him cope with his loss.

The most helpful person in Florida was Harry's neighbor, Carol. Bernice and Harry had played golf with Carol's son, Tim, and her husband Ed, when he was alive.

Harry's eyes began to twinkle as he talked about Carol. "I was beginning to realize Carol was somebody wonderful to have around," he recalled. "I think it was Carol and her sister, Glade, who got me broken away from my despair. Carol brought dinner over several times, and Carol, Glade and I went out to dinner. I started to feel that I really liked Carol."

But he was unsure of his feelings—it hadn't been that long since Bernice's passing. Harry began to fight with himself: "What do I like about Carol?" he questioned. "I thought she was beautiful, and a beautiful person. I began praying to know that my thought process about Carol was good in every way."

Prayer had always been important to Harry. Ironically, he'd been so upset about his wife's death that he hadn't prayed much—praying about his feelings for Carol actually brought "the spiritual," as he called it, back into his thinking.

Harry told me he shocked Carol by telling her he was falling in love with her. "I had been concerned that the attraction was just physical," he said. "But by the time I asked her to marry me, I was convinced it was spiritual."

"I asked her to marry me," he recalled, "and she said, 'It might be nice.'"

****

Bernice and Harry had spent nine summers in Beach Mountain, North Carolina. Bernice loved the mountains, and they had wonderful friends in Beach Mountain. "There were five or six [couples] up there who gave me a lot of support," Harry said. "I felt very, very grateful—and still do—for the friendship they expressed for me at that time." Upon his retirement from the Brunswick Corporation, where he'd been employed 37 years, Harry became involved with the Club at Beach Mountain, working with the golf course and with other club activities. After his 50th anniversary celebration, he tried to go back to the work he'd been doing up there, but he found it wasn't quite the same— his mind was still on Carol, who lived in Florida.

"About this time I realized I wanted to see more of Carol," he said. "This was about five months on. I had already asked her to marry me."

Fortunately for Harry, he and Carol had mutual friends who also summered at Beach Mountain. "We made an excuse for Carol to come up because Priscilla and Mabel were there," Harry recalled.

They got a hotel room for Carol, and Harry and Carol visited back and forth. They also had dinner with several of Harry's friends. Everyone thought a lot of Carol and tried to make her comfortable. "I sometimes took her back to her hotel late...Carol was very proper. No shenanigans," he added, smiling.

"After we came back to Florida, I was ready to re-marry, but Carol was not," Harry told me. "Certainly, for me, there was a strong love." They waited until they'd gotten past the first year of Bernice's passing, then Carol said yes, they could get married.

Harry and Carol Abbot were married in 2002.

****

The Abbotts have now been married 11 years. They are an attractive couple—both tall, elegant in appearance, and friendly to everyone. They exhibit a lively, bantering humor with each other, which is often characteristic of couples who started out as friends.

When discussing his reasons for wanting to marry Carol, Harry was adamant. "Five months after Bernice's passing, I started to feel very comfortable with another woman, and Carol was it. Also, I just didn't want to live alone. I didn't go back and forth between, 'Should I get married or shouldn't I?' It wasn't whether I should get married again; it was a natural decision. There was one other woman I thought of. She was my secretary, and she'd been supportive, but once Carol came into the picture, that disappeared."

Carol and Harry's house is full of paintings that were created by Bernice Abbott, along with pictures of both their families. "When I think back to Bernice, and my romance with her...I know I'll never experience the kind of love she had for me again, no matter what. It was absolutely unquestioned. She was so much a part of everything I did. I knew all along what a wonderful thing I had in her love."

Harry's Advice for Widowers:

"The bottom line is just recognizing the gratitude you have for your life together. Bernice's love for me was a constant thing...it is still with me."

Guidelines for Widowers

1. This is one time to listen to your children. Harry's told him to go ahead with the 50th Anniversary celebration, and it turned out to be the first step to his healing.

2. Praying about each new step in your recovery is a wonderful way to connect to the most spiritual side of you.

3. Don't be shy about involving friends in your recovery plans—Harry asked two long time pals to facilitate a visit from Carol to his North Carolina house. It worked out well—and how!

4. Realize that it may not be possible to go back to your "old life"—Harry tried working at the Club again, but it just wasn't the same. Instead, he moved forward, and eventually entered into a new relationship.

5. If you want to get married again—do so. It's nobody's business but your own.

Chapter Thirty-Four

Falling in Love Again

When our spouse dies, typically, we are devastated—we think we will never be romantically interested in another person again. Often, we retreat into ourselves and find solace by licking our wounds in any number of ways—some of which have been discussed in this book.

After a while, some men find it's just too lonely to carry on by themselves. (Not everyone feels this way, and if you're comfortable with the solo life, you can rest assured there are many other widowers who feel the same.) However, if you find yourself looking around just a bit, chances are you may be thinking about having another woman in your life. Perhaps you've already started dating or have signed up for one of the Internet dating sites mentioned earlier. Maybe you've already met someone—a woman who strikes your fancy. No, she can't replace your late wife, and you wouldn't want her to, but you like her a lot. You like being with her.

And one day, that liking turns into something else. You can't believe it's happening. You can't eat when you're around her; the two of you sit staring at each other in restaurants, your sumptuous meals untouched. You can't sleep; all you can think about is her—what is going on?

Yes, it's true—you are falling in love again. For Harry Abbot, this happened early, less than a year after his wife's passing. Unsure whether it was a physical attraction or the real thing, Harry began to pray. Prayer is certainly one way to sort out your feelings; putting your trust in God (asking for God's guidance) goes hand in hand with falling in love.

If you do fall in love, you don't necessarily have to get married right away. You can wait until you're absolutely sure, or you could not get married at all—just continue on in your blissful state of being in love, and hope that it will last.

For some men, Harry included, getting married again was exactly what they wanted to do. You know deep in your heart that your late wife only wants your happiness. If you decide to get married again, she will understand.

Love. Marriage. For some people, one great love is enough, and the memory of it will nourish them for the rest of their lives. For others, falling in love again is as natural as a walk in the park. They don't want an affair; they want the real thing—again.

Only you know what type of man you are. Remember, dear widower, you're never too old to take a risk when it comes to love.

Chapter Thirty-Five

Gratitude

While there may be times when it's hard to be grateful, the expression of gratitude is one of the most healing remedies there is for grief. When we are grateful, our heart fills with joy, and we are momentarily lifted up, out of ourselves, to a union with our Creator.

For a new widower, the expression of gratitude can be a balm against loneliness and the pain of your loss. How do we go about expressing gratitude, and what is our gratitude for?

You can start with very simple things—appreciate the fact that you had a good breakfast this morning, or that your neighbor returned your clippers the very day you wanted to trim the hedges. You can be grateful for your health, your job, and your children's well-being, and, of course, you can be grateful for all the years you spent with your beautiful wife.

How can we express this gratitude once we've begun to cultivate it (it may take a while to get it going)? You can talk about your wife with relatives and friends and tell them how much you appreciated her. Your children, especially, will be glad to hear you express gratitude for their mother and will probably join you in these reminiscences. You can make a list of all the wonderful things you and your late wife did together—trips you took, projects you embarked upon, holiday get-togethers—and you can look at photographs, by yourself or with others.

Most importantly, you can give thanks to God for letting you share those 20, 35 or 50 years with that wonderful woman. Just say, "Thank you, God!"

Chapter Thirty-Six

Change

Harry Abbott didn't have much trouble accepting change in his life, but many people do. Faced with a loss, Harry followed his heart and began a new life, making a radical change by getting married again.

Not everyone can do this, and not everyone wants to. As a new widower, you may find it easier to deal with your feelings, and all the new things that are happening to you, if you accept change.

Change is inevitable in everyone's life. As we move out of puberty and into adulthood—going to college, finding a job, and getting married—we are faced with a constant series of changes, adjustments, and new patterns in our days. For young people, accepting change comes easily—in fact, most young adults relish each new phase of their existence as they gain increased independence.

As we get older, however, it can become harder to deal with change. We get comfortable in our lifestyle; it suits us, and we want to keep it that way. Faced with a monumental challenge, such as the loss of our spouse, we're thrown off-kilter. As our old patterns and habits close down and new ones open up, we are often reluctant to embrace them, simply because they're different. We don't want to change.

But change we must, and chances are, as a new widower, you've spent the last year finding that out. You've had to establish new eating routines, new avenues for socialization, and new ways to spend your time. The more you can accept these changes, and, indeed, embrace them whenever possible, the easier your new life will be.

So look at all that has happened this past year as part of your growth process. You are becoming a wiser, more independent, and more complete individual on your own, and you are able to pursue whatever interests appeal to you, perhaps for the first time in many years. Now that's a change that ought to make you happy!

Chapter Thirty-Seven

Walter Johnson

"I figured I'd gone through it once and I'd do it again."

"I've been married twice. I lost both wives to cancer," Walter Johnson told me, with a hint of a tear in his eye. He is a lively man, optimistic and cheerful despite his losses.

"Helen died in 1993. We were married 45 years. I spent our 45th anniversary with her in the hospital," he said.

Walter and Helen raised their family—a son and a daughter—in eastern Massachusetts, about 25 miles west of Boston, where Walter worked in the industrial field. The couple was active in the Baptist Church—both were youth leaders, and Helen was the Sunday School secretary.

"I was in love with her, and I thought she was wonderful," Walter said.

Helen was diagnosed with cancer after the couple had moved South. "She had surgery, and they said if she could go three years, she'd be cured," Walter said. "She went two and a half years, and then had a check-up. They found a tumor."

Walter told me he thought his life was over when Helen died. "The first month, I did nothing. I had good neighbors—they watched over me," he said.

He was attending Church regularly and was grateful that his church friends also took care of him. The parishioners often went out to lunch after Church on Sunday, which cheered him up considerably. "If it wasn't for Church, I don't know what I would have done," he said.

It was at one of the church functions that he met his second wife, Bette.

"When I told my son on the phone that I was getting re-married, he hung up on me," Walter recalled, laughing. "But I enjoyed my marriage. People used to say to me, if I didn't have a happy marriage, I wouldn't have gotten married a second time."

Walter said his son, David, later told Bette he was glad his father had gotten married again. "He said, 'Thank you for taking care of my Dad.'"

❋❋❋❋❋❋❋❋❋❋❋❋❋

Walter and Bette got married in 1994. They led an active life as retirees. "Bette was a great bowler," Walter recalled. They participated in a number of community and church activities, but Bette began feeling unwell.

Her daughter had died a few years earlier. "She was hurt," Walter told me, attributing some of Bette's difficulties to that tragedy.

Bette was diagnosed with lung cancer around 2008. She died in April of 2010.

"What I should have done is gone to a grieving counselor right away. Not many men do that. I figured I'd gone through it once and I'd do it again," Walter said.

He had a hard time at first. Finally, he talked to a counselor through his church.

"I used to wonder why God took both wives from me," he said. "But after I talked with the counselor...I can say, 'God didn't take those ladies away from me. He gave me the honor and privilege of taking care of them in their last days and earlier.

"I don't understand how a person gets along without God."

****

Nowadays, Walter finds himself a bit "hermatized," as he put it, although he still goes bowling with his park bowling league, often taking a blind couple with him. Once a month he attends a pot-luck supper in the park, and he often goes to ice cream socials.

"Sunday is my best day of the week," he said. "I go to Sunday Church services and out to lunch afterward."

He also attends Wednesday night services and meetings of the Young at Heart club. "You look around and there's always someone worse off than you," he said, indicating that he likes to help people whenever he can.

Walter is a firm believer in prayer, and he takes it very seriously. "I don't pray enough," he confessed. "There are times when I should be praying and I don't."

He also spends a lot of time on his computer. "I got on Facebook about a year ago—I got on to see pictures of my great grandson," he said. "I had about 150 of those within a year." On Facebook, he's "friends" with his son's and daughter's families and also with some of the people from his old youth group in Massachusetts.

"My youth group is all of retirement age now," Walter said.

He is 88 years old but he still says, "I don't give up. I might find another person. I've been told a couple of times, 'Never say never.'

"In fact, I have a kind of date this Sunday after Church," he added, smiling. "So that's good."

Walter's Advice to Widowers

"The way I look at things now—I'm trying to leave everything in God's hands."

Guidelines for Widowers.

1. Walter credits his Church with pulling him out of the doldrums after his first wife died. If you don't go to Church, this might be a good time to try it.

2. After his second wife died, Walter considered going to a counselor but didn't do it right away. When he finally did talk to someone, it was helpful—and he was grateful.

3. Think about helping others who might be even worse off than you—this is a form of "distraction" that works wonders.

4. Join Facebook! You're never too old to share family pictures, are you?

5. Above all, if you'd like to be with another person, don't give up. As Walter says, "Never say never!"

Chapter Thirty-Eight

Optimism

Walter Johnson likes to keep an optimistic point of view on his life, and you should too. Good things have a way of happening to people who expect good to be waiting right around the corner. Often, we'll find that something we've been picturing in our mind will suddenly appear—whether you call it magic or synchronicity, a hopeful attitude often brings unexpected and welcome results.

Would you like another person in your life to fill the void left by your wife's passing? Would you like more friends, more sociable neighbors, or maybe a new activity to fill your day? Even if you don't have a clue right now of how to achieve this desire (even, in fact, if you don't know what the "new activity" you want is)—keep an open, optimistic frame of mind on the subject. Look for signs of God's goodness—a beautiful afternoon when you'd planned to go for a walk in the park, a sale on computers at WalMart the very day you decided to purchase one—and be thankful for your good fortune. You can even keep a list of the good things that happen to you—you'll be surprised how the list seems to expand exponentially the more you work on it.

So, court optimism if at all possible, and watch the blessings begin to flow. Chances are the very thing you've been envisioning will soon be on your list of "good things" that have happened to you.

****

Chapter Thirty Nine

The Whole Man

What does it mean to be a complete human being, one who has gained an acceptance of himself and his current condition? As a widower, you may find this hard to answer, because any state of acceptance or satisfaction may seem, at best, temporary. A part of you always seems to be waiting, even though, after a year, you are not quite sure what it is you're waiting for.

Your physical senses, including sight, touch, and smell—even memories and transitory feelings—are always reminding you that you are alone, that your spouse is no longer with you. You may marry again or find a relationship with another person for a time, but ultimately, you will probably discover that you must locate happiness and satisfaction within you.

The peace with and acceptance of who you really are ultimately has little to do with another person. In essence, it is a realization that you can love yourself just the way God loves you. You can appreciate your own experiences and your own qualities of patience, tolerance, gratitude and optimism, which you have cultivated this year as a widower. No, you are not the same—you are more. You have become a whole man, not dependent on another individual for happiness or for giving meaning to your existence, but strong and fully sufficient to carry on in life.

So pat yourself on the back for all you've accomplished this year. As your life continues to unfold, new and glorious experiences will appear, which will certainly enrich your soul.

Chapter Forty

The Awakening

At some point, dear widower, you will look around you and realize that the worst part of your mourning is behind you. It may happen at nine months, or it may take you two years or more to achieve this feeling, but achieve it you will. It's not that you've forgotten your wife—you will never forget her. You will probably continue to miss her, and you'll no doubt think of her every day. However, the pain has lessened. You no longer want to stay in bed all day, and you can do things for yourself that make you feel good: go to a ballgame, for example, or spend the day at the beach or golf course, or at the lake with your fishing pole.

Maybe you've found another person to share your days with; maybe you're even contemplating marriage—if so, you will move out of the rank of widower and into the role of "husband" once again. Even if you haven't met anyone with whom you'd like to share the rest of your life, or you've decided you're doing just fine on your own—the change is there. Other people notice it; they no longer approach you with a look of concern on their faces. Instead, they pat you on the shoulder and say, "How's it going?" as if you're just any old Joe, enjoying your life.

And the funny thing is, you have begun to enjoy life again. You were amazed at the level of energy in your limbs as you moved that piece of lawn furniture this morning, and this afternoon, in the car, a song on the radio, an oldie goldie, made you hum along and tap the steering wheel in time to the beat. That surprised you—that unexpected feeling of being "young" again, as if all this tragedy never happened.

This is the "awakening"—that moment when you realize you still have a life to live, and you're happy about that.

Your love for your late wife will always be there for you. Wherever she is, she will continue to love you, as you love her. But for right now—there's a few things left you'd like to do, a few places you'd like to go. Amazingly, you have the energy, the desire and the enthusiasm to do just that.

Welcome to your new life, dear widower. May it bring you the peace of mind, comfort and pleasure you deserve!

Index

M

marriage 126
marriage vow 62
massage 52
Match.com 90
memory 22, 34, 89, 97, 113, 126
Monk, Adrian 61, 62
movie 49, 56, 68, 80, 115
music 23, 25, 45, 71, 73, 84, 86, 90, 93, 106
musical instruments 53

N

NASCAR 15
Navy 57, 97
Netflix 67
New Year's Eve 26
New York Times 56, 58, 59, 79, 116
Nicholson, Jack 49
nursing home 70, 84, 94

O

one day at a time 29, 30
optimism viii, 135

P

passionate 83, 86, 93, 94
pets 65, 100, 102
phone 16, 17, 50, 56, 57, 58, 63, 64, 65, 75, 114, 132
photographs 98, 113, 114, 128
plant 18, 32, 52
poetry 57, 59, 79
power walking 41, 42, 94
prayer 18, 29, 45, 46, 47, 71, 72, 73, 84, 98, 108, 133
Psalm, 23rd 46
Psalm, 91st 47

Praise for Joanna Romer's Widow: A Survival Guide for the First Year

"...a notable self-help guide that would offer knowledge, experience, and insight for others facing a similar situation. Romer's Widow is a practical compendium that covers all the critical issues a newly widowed spouse will face....Clearly the author writes from a heartfelt place. Her words stem not merely from a sympathetic point of view, but seem more suggestive of a desire to share wisdom...Ideally readers will come away from this work considering the author and her survival guide as significant new friends."

-Carol Davala, *The U.S. Review of Books*

"...Having this book by my bedside has been such a comfort. It's not the type of book you just read once and put away. No, I reach for it time and time again as new situations come up or just to reassure myself that what I'm feeling is normal."

-*The Daytona Beach News-Journal*

"Joanna Romer knows just what to say in 48 short chapters addressed to women who are accustomed to thinking of themselves as wives, but who now must learn what it means to live as another "w" word, widow. Any widow could benefit from reading this book...

-johnfgaines, *Library Thing*

"Widow: A Survival Guide for the First Year is a self-help and inspirational guide for those who are coping with the loss of a soulmate. Advising how to best cope with the emotional overload, dealing with practical matters such as the leftovers of physical possession, and most importantly, finding the way to keep living life when it seems like the last thing you want to do. Widow is a powerful and much recommended addition to self-help collections..."

-Reviewer's Choice, *Midwest Book Review*

"Written in an easy, practical style, Widow is a wonderful resource for anyone who has lost a spouse."

-*The Villager*

Other Books by MSI Press

Thoughts without a Title

Understanding the People Around You: An Introduction to Socionics

What Works: Helping Students Reach Native-like Second-Language Competence

When You're Shoved from the Right, Look to the Left: Metaphors of Islamic Humanism

Working with Advanced Foreign Language Students

Journal for Distinguished Language Studies (annual issue)

CPSIA information can be obtained at www.ICGtesting.com
Printed in the USA
LVOW04s2308051014

407390LV00010B/65/P